Soul
Pain

SOUL PAIN

EXPOSING THE VALUELESS LIE

By

Dr. Roger L. Frye

LATTE **Brothers**
COMMUNICATIONS

Published by:
Latte Brothers Communications Press
1030 E. Hwy 377 Suite 110 Box 184
Granbury, TX 76048
All Rights Reserved

ISBN-978-0-9834869-0-9

Endorsements

Soul Pain is an easy to read book that describes various Spirit-anointed prayer approaches for healing the pains within our souls. The book is full of stories so you will easily find your life story within its pages. The healing prayers and worksheets within the book make each chapter instantly applicable to healing any wounds that have been uncovered through the chapter. You will find healing from traumas, abandonment, rejection, victimization, isolation, pride, and many other wounds within your soul. Innovative prayer ministries, such as inner healing and deliverance are woven together with Biblical meditations and confessions to help you experience quick release from your pain. You will find healing within these pages!!!

Dr. Mark Virkler

Author of "4 Keys to Hearing God's Voice" and President of Christian Leadership University

Dr. Roger Frye's latest book, *Soul Pain, Exposing the Valueless Lie,* is a powerful and effective standout that delivers gems of teaching in a winsome and easily owned format.

In Jeremiah 8:11, God speaks of those who exercise superficial ministry as missing the mark. He says, "They have lightly healed" which is inadequate. It is especially so for some of those with whom the Church ministers. People come with broken lives and they are often given band-aids or platitudes. In *Soul Pain*, Roger provides the tools to transform broken lives and free shackled hearts; and does it in a way that provides step by step help to realize healing.

While *Soul Pain* is a must for the broken, it is also a great tool for anyone who wants to find God's best for their life. This book is a ministry that will help people soak in God's healing pool and experience the Father's love, apply the Son's victory, and walk in the Holy Spirit's power.

The Rt. Rev. Dr. Bill Atwood

Bishop of The International Diocese, ACNA
~ Suffragan Bishop for International Affairs
All Saints Cathedral Diocese, Nairobi
Anglican Church of Kenya

I have witnessed the freeing up of many lives over the years by Roger Frye's ministry. This book will be a help not only for the wounded souls but also for those who love them. It builds from a sure foundation in scripture, has lots of illustrations and humor. This is a very practical book, with examples of prayers and lots of other resources for helping and receiving help. I recommend this book to pastors who care about the souls of their people, to those with wounded souls in need of healing, and to those that think they don't deserve healing.

John Clifford

Pastor
Faith Church -Anglican

Roger Frye does a very good job of dealing with the subject of "SOUL PAIN". He goes into great detail of how to recognize the valueless lie in your life and how to overcome it. He gives many illustrations on how it works in your life. No one who reads this book should remain in a valueless state or under the control of this lie. The book will serve as a road map to freedom from being used and kept in the dark as you learn how such a lie works.

Dr. Henry Malone

Author of "Shadow Boxing"
and President and founder of Vision Life Ministries

Testimonies of those receiving the Valuelessness Strongman Ministry

In his valueless strongman ministry, Roger uses a very systematic, thorough approach in identifying key lies which might block (either fully or partially) a person's experience of the love of God. This identification becomes the key to unlocking God's heart and God's thoughts concerning these lies. When God speaks to a person's inner beliefs about himself, things change and transformation takes place.

That was certainly my experience. Within a week after going through Roger's ministry approach, I felt major transformation. Why did it take a week? Because, in my case, the deliverance (which Roger does following the processing of lies) was so extensive and effective, it took some time for the dust to clear out.

Roger's valueless strongman ministry is a great approach to ministry and it gets right at the heart of man's dilemma—his need to experience the love of God in its fullness. I highly recommend Roger's valueless strongman ministry.

V.C.

During my first personal session with Pastor Frye, he observed "valuelessness" in many of my responses and recommended a second session. I had no idea what he meant, but quickly agreed. He had stirred something in me and I felt wonderful. If he thought we could improve upon that, I was ready.

While driving to our second meeting, I realized I had some rebellion in my heart toward God. Pastor Frye asked me why I thought the Holy Spirit had brought that to my attention—and why I had been urged to bring it to his attention. Follow-up questions led me back to my childhood relationship with my father. Dad had been a Jekyll and Hyde: life of the party one minute; overbearing and threatening the next. Looking back, I realize that schoolwork came rather easily to me—with little effort or studying—but my dad had often called me a "dumb, damn kid." As an impressionable boy, I accepted his angry critiques without question: I was dumb—valueless.

Pastor Frye worked with me to forgive my father and myself for the inner vows and judgments I had made against my father and, once again, I was deeply stirred and relieved. I left feeling light, happy and peaceful. Pastor Frye knows what he is talking about.

M. S.

Growth happens in my life when I'm challenged to look honestly and deeply inside my heart and soul and respond to God's healing touch. In the ministry appointment, I quickly understood that some of my deepest pains, beliefs and struggles were a result of the valueless strongman. As I went through these lies, God showed me new truths that will forever change how I see myself, others and God. The deliverance part brought freedom to a deep part of my heart that had been locked away and is now free.

C. B.

Suffering physical and emotional trauma at the age of 9 set me on a path of shame and self hatred. Inner healing and deliverance have brought great freedom to my life. Walking it out is a continual process which brought me to a deeper level of addressing the lies of the enemy that I had been believing. The valueless ministry described in *Soul Pain* has produced in me the literal sensation of being free of a weight upon my chest and within my heart. Comprehending where Jesus was in those difficult moments of life, and what He has to say to us about them, brings tangible relief and peace.

S.B.

Many years later after much ministry for sexual abuse (which was quite freeing), anger still continued to surface in me and I had now moved into my 50's. As this strong anger continued to surface I couldn't imagine what it could possibly be especially after years of ministry for the abuse. A friend told me about Roger and that I must go see him. She took me to him. The Holy Spirit led him for 7 hours taking me through conception, 9 months in the womb and my birth with quite a bit of forgiveness - tons and tons of anger was released. I was overwhelmed with the liberty that came and freedom from this "gripping" anger. I am still amazed and relieved - very grateful and overwhelmed with God's extreme love and mercy. Too deep and too much for any words.

J.R.

I dedicate this book to my mother, who prayed for me daily for many years and who served as an example of Christian commitment and love for the Lord. She overcame very difficult circumstances to live as a faithful follower of Jesus Christ and a person of influence in the Christian community in which she joyously labored throughout the years. She will always be fondly remembered by those whose lives she touched.

Disclaimer

Soul Pain does not seek to be in conflict with any medical or psychiatric practices. The information here is intended for your spiritual growth and general knowledge. It is not intended to be a substitute for medical or psychiatric advice or treatment for specific medical or psychological conditions or disorders.

Foreward

As I read through the manuscript of *SOUL PAIN* my heart was made to rejoice because someone was addressing this lie in a very powerful way. I came to realize that so many people are ruled by this lie. There are thousands of souls out there that can benefit from this work.

It is a must read book because you may find yourself in its pages. Many do not even know that they suffer at the hands of such a deceptive spirit. The spirit of valuelessness is widespread and most of those suffering from it do not know it.

Roger Frye does a very good job of dealing with the subject of *SOUL PAIN*. He goes into great detail of how to recognize the valueless lie in your life and how to overcome it. He gives many illustrations on how it works in your life. No one who reads this book should remain in a valueless state or under the control of this lie. The book will serve as a road map to freedom from being used and kept in the dark as you learn how such a lie operates.

It has been a joy to speak into the lives of Roger and Ruth for some time now. You will not be disappointed when you read this book. I could hardly put it down. It is interesting and challenging to read. So sit back and enjoy yourself. Let God move in your life in a powerful way.

Dr. Henry Malone
Vision Life Ministries
Lewisville, Texas

Contents

Acknowledgments

I wish to express my deepest gratitude to Bob Lee, Fran Kennedy-Ellis and Aaron Mitchell for their work in editing the rough draft of this book. I thank them for their supportive role in completing the book.

I want to say thank you to my dear friends, Dennis and Elena Dotson, who recently encouraged me to write another book.

I am grateful for the team members at Tom Mawman's Prophetic School who encouraged me to write. Their words motivated me to take up again the task of writing, which I had put on the back burner for quite some time.

I want to thank Sheree Bates for her assistance in editing and proofreading the final draft. I am also deeply appreciative to my other friends who offered insightful comments.

I want to acknowledge the special friends at Vision Life Ministries who have helped hone my skills in ministering to people to help them get free from the bondages of the past.

I want to acknowledge the special friends and partners who contributed financially to underwrite the publication of this book. Thank you for being willing to invest in the lives of people who will be benefited by reading and applying its principles.

And finally, special thanksgiving goes to my Pastor, John Clifford, and the dear members of Faith Church. Their unwavering support has significantly impacted my life and without their help I would not have been able to write this book.

Introduction

The term "soul pain" is not used here in a technical Biblical sense, in that the soul is distinct from the human spirit and the body. What I mean to communicate by this title is that pain lodges down deep within the person and affects his/her entire being. The pain enters through a traumatic experience and then sustains itself when a person believes a lie(s) about himself.

Through many years of ministering to people I have discovered that approximately forty percent of those who I counsel have been told the basic lie that they are of no intrinsic value. Many of these folks, who are Christians, know what the Bible says in this regard—that they are of utmost worth to God. They know with head-knowledge that they are of such great value to our Heavenly Father that He sent His Son, Jesus, to die on the cross to save them from sin so that they might become a part of His spiritual family forever. They know that oft-quoted Scripture, *For God so loved the world that He gave His only begotten Son...* (John 3:16), but when the rubber meets the road, when the pressures of life press them in, their reactions reveal their heart-belief that they are, in fact, of no intrinsic value. I call this the *valueless lie*.

The valueless lie is also an antichrist spirit. It is an antichrist spirit because it contravenes the incalculable worth God has placed in every individual through Christ's sacrificial death on the cross. In some respects it is similar to the spirit of rejection only it runs deeper and has a more profound stranglehold on its victim. Rejection and valuelessness usually go hand-in-hand except that rejection has more to do with what is *done* to you or what you *do* to others, whereas, the valueless lie has to do with *who you are* as a person. Valuelessness flows from the rejection received from a lie. A person often concludes that because he/she is rejected they are of no value.

The most common way a person receives the valueless lie is through the woundings of the heart. A traumatic experience that causes inner wounds provides fertile soil for the enemy to implant lies that tear down the worth of the individual. I believe the valueless spirit can also be passed down to us genetically from our ancestors. Along with the basic lie of "I'm of no value," the devil seeks to imbed what I call subsidiary lies. Below is a list of common subsidiary lies but there are probably many more. Read through the list. Be honest with yourself and check off any of these lies you believe you received at some time in your life.

    __"If I perform well I will be loved and accepted."
    __"My worth is in what I do."
    __"I must reject others before they reject me."
    __"I'm a burden."
    __"I'm an intrusion."
    __"Something is wrong with me."
    __"I'll never get anything right."
    __"I'm the reason my parents can't get along."
    __"It's my fault my parents divorced or died."
    __"I am alone."
    __"No one will support me."
    __"I have to depend on myself."
    __"I don't belong."
    __"No one cares how I feel."
    __"No one will listen to me."
    __"No one will love me just for who I am."
    __"If I isolate myself I won't get hurt."
    __"I am a bad person."
    __"My best effort is never good enough."
    __"If I avoid conflict I won't be rejected."

___ "If I were a male/female I would be of more value."
___ "I will never change into God's design for my life."
___ "I am unattractive."
___ "I'm a mistake."
___ "The other person is always right and I'm always wrong."
___ "I will always be by myself."
___ "No one will protect me."
___ "No one will help me."
___ "I'm not lovable."
___ "I am inadequate."
___ "I'm not as good as everyone else."
___ "I must be what others want me to be."
___ "If I'm invisible I won't be hurt."
___ "God won't protect me."
___ "What I have to say is of no value."
___ "My gifts and talents are inferior to others."
___ "It would be better if I were dead."
___ "Anything that is given to me will be taken away."
___ "Girls/boys aren't important."
___ "I am not wanted."
___ "I will always be abandoned."
___ "I will always be left out."
___ "No one will mentor me."
___ "I am doomed to fail."
___ "My actions will never be appreciated."
___ "I'm a loser."
___ "The only thing I'm good for is sex."
___ "I will never get ahead."
___ "I will always struggle financially."
___ "Everything I cherish will be taken from me."

Now count the number you checked off. If you marked even one, that lie needs to be dealt with. If you marked more than ten, the valueless lie runs especially deep in your life. But the good news is Jesus wants to set you free!

Lies always lead to bondage but the truth always leads to freedom. That is why Jesus said, *Ye shall know the truth and the truth shall make you free* (John 8:32, KJV). The word "know" in the original language refers to an experiential knowledge—it is that which we know in the depths of our being. To obtain a mere head-knowledge about our inherent worth will not lead to true freedom. There must be a truth encounter whereby the Spirit of the living God intersects our human spirit, revealing truth to our inner man.

We must bring our thinking into conformity with what God says about us. Whether we want to admit it or not, we are in a spiritual battle against the devil. The main strategy that he uses to wage war against us centers around our thought life. The apostle Paul warned us, *For though we live in the world, we do not wage war as the world does. The weapons we fight with are not the weapons of the world. On the contrary, they have divine power to demolish strongholds. We demolish arguments and every pretension that sets itself up against the knowledge of God, and we take captive every thought to make it obedient to Christ* (2 Corinthians 10:3-5, NIV).

Another interesting observation I have made is that those infected by the valueless spirit also have a hard time trusting God. My experience in ministering to hundreds of people and hearing their stories is that almost all of them who have believed the lie that they are of no intrinsic value have also believed the lie that God is not good. I have never known a follower of Christ to hold to the theological position in their mind that God is not good. However, when it comes to the heart, this lie runs deep. It is the same basic lie that Satan foisted on Eve in the Garden of Eden and it is the lie that he has been feeding people ever since.

For those who have not accepted their intrinsic worth, the logic of this lie is simple. If you believe that you are of no inherent value, and you believe that God created you, then logically, God is not good. If God is not good then He cannot be trusted. You have to fend for yourself because God is withholding from you those good things you desperately need.

The valueless spirit opens a person up to a host of other problems. One of the opposites of trust is fear. If you have a hard time trusting God you will tend to have difficulty letting go of your fears. You need to know how valuable you are to Almighty God, your Creator and Sustainer. Only then will you have the firm foundation upon which faith can grow strong. *There is no fear in love; but perfect love casteth out fear: because fear hath torment. He that feareth is not made perfect in love* (1 John 4:18, KJV).

Another problem is that the valueless spirit opens the door to autoimmune diseases whereby the body literally attacks itself. It's as if the immune system begins to listen to the individual's heart and taps into its flawed belief system. The body's immune system receives the message that, because the person is of no value, it needs to be destroyed. People who suffer from autoimmune diseases and other chronic diseases can greatly benefit from applying the principles found in this book. It is not the only answer but I believe it is "one piece of the pie" to help us in receiving healing.

Additionally, the lies one believes become expectations. Expectations are a negative form of faith—they project onto one's self, other people, and life circumstances, releasing a negative spiritual energy to ensure that they be realized. For example, if I expect to be rejected by people, I will receive an inordinate amount of rejection because I will draw it to myself like a magnet. If I expect that people won't like me, I will attract that type of behavior from others. This dynamic explains why some people who have adopted these negative expectancies believe that they are in fact the truth, not lies. They have experienced these lies being played out over and over again.

When I refer to the "valueless spirit" the term actually deals with two different realities. On the one hand there are spirit beings that afflict individuals and cause particular adverse consequences. On the other hand, there is a distinct way of thinking that people can develop quite apart from evil spirits. The term "valueless spirit" is used rather loosely to describe a demonic strongman as well as a mind-set in a person.

Throughout this book I use stories to illustrate the cause and effect of the valueless spirit. These stories are derived from a compilation of ministry experiences. With the exception of personal anecdotes, the names and many of the details of the stories have been changed to protect the privacy of the individuals.

God desires that His people live in joy and peace, but to live life to its fullest we must rid our hearts of the valueless spirit. This insidious spirit holds on tenaciously to its victims and does not leave without a fight. It usually seems to leave in stages as the individual repents for coming into agreement with any of its subsidiary lies and as they renew their mind. Don't approach the valuelessness in your life expecting a quick fix. Determine to contend for your freedom, doing whatever it takes, and you will begin to live in ever-increasing levels of victory.

1

In Utero Wounds

S ome of the wounds we experience happen to us even before we are born. Wounds that take place while we are yet in our mother's womb can be some of the most difficult to heal because obviously, we have no conscious memory of their occurrence. For example, when a pregnant woman takes a drink of alcohol her unborn child takes the same drink. Whatever she eats or drinks during her pregnancy goes directly through her bloodstream, through the placenta and into the baby. It is common knowledge that alcohol interferes with the child's ability to get enough oxygen and nourishment for the cells in the brain and other organs to develop normally. The unborn child has little tolerance for alcohol and can develop serious problems. In the same way that the mother's dietary habits affect the child, the mother's emotional responses influence the baby in her womb as well.

His Parents Didn't Want Any More Children

Stephen's parents already had four small children when his natural mother, Michelle, received a positive pregnancy test result. "Oh no," she complained to Ron, her husband, "Not another baby.

We can't afford it! And besides our car is full as it is and there wouldn't be room for another car seat."

With her husband's consent, and because she didn't want to have to pay for an abortion, she decided to put the baby into the state-run foster care program. Based on their financial situation it would be easy, according to their state's regulations, to simply turn the infant over to the child protective services once he was born. A friend found out about Michelle's plan and told her that she knew of a wonderful Christian couple, Fred and Amy, who had been seeking for over a year to adopt a child. Fred and Amy had pursued various avenues of adoption, one being an Indian agency, but had run into a lot of graft and bureaucratic red tape and were becoming quite discouraged.

Through her friend's urging, Michelle finally contacted Fred and Amy. However, instead of caring whether or not the baby was placed in a loving stable home, Michelle concerned herself more with whatever was easiest for her. It took a lot less effort to simply give the child over to the government agency that was present right there in the county hospital. To get Michelle to make the effort to drive the forty-five miles to the county courthouse to file the legal documents meant that Fred and Amy had to give her gas and food money. They also bought some expensive gifts for her that served sort of as a bribe to prod her into filling out the necessary paperwork. Through much effort, Fred and Amy were finally able to adopt Stephen and take him home with them from the hospital after his birth. They were thrilled to have their little son and doted over him constantly.

While the above scenario was being played out, what was going on in Stephen's human spirit? Think of the deep rejection he must have felt knowing his natural parents didn't want to bother with him. Even though today he is being reared by loving adoptive parents, the damage was already done while he was still in the womb. No matter how much healthy love Fred and Amy demonstrate, the devil's lies have already been implanted in his heart. The enemy no doubt took advantage of his dysfunctional family of origin situation to tell Stephen that he has no intrinsic value.

Is it too late for Stephen to gain a godly view of himself? Absolutely not! But just pouring love on him is not the answer. Many such couples have led lives of frustration due to the fact that their adopted children cannot respond positively to their love. Along with love and wholesome child rearing techniques adoptive parents must learn to deal decisively with the valueless strongman. How do they do that? I would advise them to spend a concerted season of prayer asking God to pull the pain of rejection out of the child's heart. For younger children lay your hands on the heart area while the child sleeps and ask Jesus to heal the trauma and mend the broken heart. Then pray something like this: "In Jesus' name I command the valueless spirit to go to dry places along with all of its underlings and associates including abandonment and rejection." Speak with authority to the spirit reminding it that it was defeated by Jesus' finished work on the cross. You don't need to raise your voice and startle the child. Demons respond to one's authority in Christ, not to their volume. If you feel uncomfortable praying in this manner, find an experienced prayer minister to assist.

Regularly speak to the child's human spirit words of love and affirmation. Say something like this: "Stephen, I speak the peace of God to your spirit. I say to you that you are wanted and highly valued. God's eyes were on you when you were being formed in your mother's womb. You are a delight to God and to me. God chose you to be born at this time in history and He has great plans for your life." The infant cannot comprehend what you are saying because their brain is not developed but their human spirit is fully able to drink in your words for spiritual nourishment and healing.

The Entry of Lies

Jerri made an appointment to see me because she wanted freedom from a nearly debilitating lack of confidence and insecurity that had plagued her most of her life. As we progressed with the ministry session I asked her to talk to me about her life, beginning with her earliest memories. "Were you a wanted pregnancy," I inquired?

"No, actually my parents married at a very young age. I was born seven months after the wedding to my mom who was 18 and my dad who was 19. To support his new family dad had to go to work in his father's automotive repair shop, interrupting his plans to go to college to be a veterinarian," she replied.

I explained to Jerri that the human spirit is fully aware of its surroundings at the moment of conception. John the Baptist as a baby in his mother Elizabeth's womb, leapt with joy when Mary, who was pregnant with Jesus, approached them. The unborn baby John sensed when he was in the presence of the Son of God.

"If your human spirit was completely aware of the reactions and attitudes of your parents at the time of your conception, what do you suppose would have been the lie you received about yourself?" I probed.

"What do you mean?" She responded with a quizzical expression.

I explained that when children go through trauma, Satan takes advantage of the opportunity and seeks to implant a lie in their heart. "What lie do you suppose the enemy placed in your heart while you were still in your mother's womb?" I continued.

As her eyes misted up she responded softly, "I'm an intrusion."

"How does it feel to be an intrusion?"

"Not good. It makes me feel sad."

"We know that you are not an intrusion to God. He planned for you to be on planet earth at this exact time in history. He knew the very parents through whom you would be born. He chose the very egg and sperm that would come together to form you. Right, Jerri?"

"Yes, I believe that."

"So we know that the message the devil fed you while you were still in your mother's womb was a ludicrous lie don't we?"

"Yes, it was."

"Let me read a passage of Scripture. I know you know this stuff but let these words sink into your heart. This is Psalm 139 from the Contemporary English Version. *You are the one who put me together inside my mother's body, and I praise you because of the wonderful way you created me. Everything you do is marvelous! Of this I have no doubt. Nothing about me is hidden from you! I was secretly woven together deep in the earth below, but with your own eyes you saw my body being formed. Even before I was born, you had written in your book everything I would do. Your thoughts are far beyond my understanding, much more than I could ever imagine. I try to count your thoughts, but they outnumber the grains of sand on the beach And when I awake, I will find you nearby. How I wish that you would kill all cruel and heartless people and protect me from them!* So we know, based on the Word of God, that you are not an intrusion. You were planned in the mind of God," I said as I intently looked into her eyes, "You are not an intrusion." As she began to receive those words tears flowed down her cheeks. I said it again, "You are not an intrusion." I waited a few minutes before continuing.

"So what is the lie behind the lie that you are an intrusion?"

"What do you mean?" She asked, revealing a tint of confusion through her facial expression.

"I believe that there is another lie behind this lie." Then I prayed out loud, "Lord, take Jerri to the original lie."

"I don't belong, is what is coming up in my mind," she responded.

"OK, if you don't belong, how does that feel?" I asked empathetically.

"It feels like there is something wrong with me but I know that's not true."

"You know, based on the Word of God, that God doesn't make any junk. But in your heart of hearts you believed the lie that the devil implanted in you. So would you say that you believed the lie that there is something wrong with you?"

"Yes, I believe I did."

"How does that feel?"

"Horrible."

"You feel horrible. If you could paint a picture of what you are feeling, what would that picture look like?" I asked, wanting her to verbalize her emotions.

"It would be a picture that is almost entirely black with a little gray around the edges."

"What is the lie behind this lie?" "Lord, take Jerri back to the original lie," I interrupted with another prayer. "If something is wrong with you, if you don't belong, if you are an intrusion, what does this say about who you are as a person?"

"That I'm not good for anything," she replied with more tears streaming down her face.

"If you're not good for anything then you are of no value. You are worthless, right?"

"Yes," she sobbed.

Discovering the basic lie and some of the subsidiary lies proved to be key to Jerri's healing. I led her through some of the inner healing exercises and over the next several months a new confidence and poise came into her life. Even those around her could not help but notice the change.

Jerri's case typifies many who have endured in utero woundings. There are various ways in which wounds come to the heart of the unborn child. For instance, let's suppose a woman becomes deathly ill at the point of her pregnancy and is confined to bed rest until the baby is born. What message does the baby's human spirit sometimes receive in such a case? She believes that she's a nuisance or that she will cause others to suffer, and, therefore, is inherently bad.

Or let's suppose that upon receiving the news that his wife is pregnant, the husband carries on a tirade because he is convinced that they cannot afford another baby at this time. The new financial challenges lead to the couple arguing about how to spend their money. In this scenario what message often penetrates the heart of the child? He is apt to believe that he is the reason his parents can't get along and that he is a bad person. The kingdom of evil is right there to take advantage of such a situation and whisper in the heart of the child lies that devalue.

Wounds that occur at an early age tend to, but not always, impact our lives more powerfully than wounds that take place later in life. I always ask about the conditions surrounding the pregnancy in order to help uncover some of the entry points for the wounds of the heart.

He Was Conceived Out of Wedlock

Sean's parents, Greg and Joanna were sexually active prior to their marriage. In fact the reason they moved up the date of the wedding was largely due to Joanna's surprise pregnancy. It wasn't that they didn't want kids; it was just that they had hoped to wait several years so that they could get more financially settled.

When Sean came to me for ministry at age 42, he confided that he struggled to find intimacy with God. It was hard for him to enter into the Presence of the Lord. At his church he saw how others worshipped and reveled in the manifest Presence of God and he longed to have that same kind of experience. With pure determination he attended several worship conferences and even read three books on the subject but no matter how hard he tried, he always struggled to enter into true spiritual worship of Almighty God. Frustrated in his efforts to encounter God, he concluded that something must be inherently wrong with him.

I asked him if he also had a hard time connecting with groups of people. "Do you often feel like you are on the outside looking in?"

"Yes, how do you know that?" He responded with surprise.

"Apparently you have the curse of illegitimacy working in your life," I explained. "It doesn't mean that God didn't want you on planet earth at this time in history. It simply means that you or one of your ancestors was conceived out of wedlock. In the book of Deuteronomy chapter twenty-three it says, *One of illegitimate birth shall not enter the assembly of the LORD; even to the tenth generation none of his descendants shall enter the assembly of the LORD* (Deut. 23:2, NKJV)."

"This is one curse that goes back ten generations. So if one of your ancestors ten generations ago was conceived out of wedlock it could possibly have an adverse affect on you today. In the Old Testament an 'illegitimate' child could not worship with the other Israelites. They had to stay in the outer courts with the Gentiles. They were never allowed to be priests who could proceed into the Holy Place. They were on the outside looking in. We have found that 'illegitimate' children tend to have a hard time connecting with God. They can't get in to the 'inner court' so to speak. They often feel like they are on the outside looking in and cannot connect with the people of God," I explained, using our time to do a little teaching.

"How do I get this curse out of my life then?" He asked eagerly.

"Let me lead you through a prayer Sean. I ask that you pray this prayer from your heart and don't merely repeat some words. OK? Say this with me out loud from your heart;"

> *"Heavenly Father, I confess that the curse of illegitimacy operates in me and my bloodline. I hold the Blood of the Cross between me and illegitimacy. I declare that this curse is broken off of me by the Blood of Jesus for 10 generations back. I renounce all division, separation, confusion and error that*

came with illegitimacy. I receive the Spirit of Adoption as a son of God and declare that it will not murder my destiny. I ask now Father to be reconnected to you. I declare all of this is done in Jesus' Name by the power of the Blood of the Cross. Amen!" [i]

I led him through the prayer phrase-by-phrase as he repeated after me.

Then I laid my hand on him and gently prayed, "Sean, I pull you into the Beloved. I pull you into the inner court, where the Lord is. You are no longer in the outer court. I pull you in where you belong." Tears brimmed his eyes and in my spirit I sensed a shift in his heart. He also knew something had changed so I said, "Welcome home son."

Illegitimacy is not only a curse, it is also a source of wounding while we are yet in our mother's womb. Satan lies to us and tells us that we don't belong. If in our heart of hearts we have believed this insidious lie, we will experience difficulty later on in life connecting with God and/or with the Body of Christ. Even if we are not sure that we or one of our ancestors going back ten generations was conceived out of wedlock, if the *fruit* is there, the *root* is most likely there. If the fruit of illegitimacy (having difficulty connecting with God, feeling like you are on the outside looking in) is present in your life, I recommend that you pray the above prayer with an experienced prayer minister.

Healing in the Womb

Sam suffered greatly from the valueless spirit due to the rejection he received while in his mother's womb. I asked him if I could take him back into his mother's womb and with his permission we proceeded.

"Sam, in the name of Jesus, I take you back inside your mother's womb. Close your eyes and see yourself there. Jesus, take him back into his mother's womb. Sam, you are in the first month of pregnancy. I bless the sperm and the egg. I bless the newly formed cell that was the result of that union. In the first month, what do you feel?"

"Nothing really," he responded seeming puzzled by my question.

"Okay, I pull you up to the second month. What are you sensing?"

"Fear. I'm afraid," Sam replied.

"What is that fear like? Do you have a sense as to where it's coming from?"

"I'm not wanted. I get the sense that there is imminent danger. I think my mother wanted to abort me," his voice was shaking and he was visibly upset.

"Do you know that for a fact? Did your mother ever tell you that?"

"Not in so many words, but she did tell me that I was a mistake. She said I was her surprise child. I was born ten years after my only sibling," he confided.

"What was the lie the enemy placed in your little heart at that time?"

"That I'm not wanted. That I'm a mistake. That I'm better off dead," he answered with tears flowing down his cheeks.

Looking in his eyes I said, "Sam, now we know that is a ludicrous lie." The enemy lied to you. God planned for you to be born. He chose the very egg and the sperm from your mom and dad. He planned for you to be alive on earth at this time in history. Do you believe that?"

"Yes, I believe it here," pointing to his head.

I continued to tell him the truth of God's Word that God planned the moment of his conception. Finally the truth seemed to penetrate his heart and he broke down weeping, wailing and moaning. (Not everyone responds with such great emotion.) I gave him a hug and continued to say that God planned him, that he was no mistake. I led him to renounce the lies he received. I asked him if he could sense Jesus' presence with him in the womb. He told me he perceived Jesus there persuading his mother not to abort him. I led him to ask Jesus if He wanted him to be born. Through the ears of his heart he heard the Lord say a resounding yes!

"How does that feel?"

"Wonderful!" He responded with a bright smile on his face.

I commanded the spirit of fear and the death curse to leave him that came in as a result of his mother planning to abort him. "I speak blessings over you in the second month," I continued. Now I pull you up into the third month. In the third month what are you sensing?"

"Peace. I feel like my mother has emotionally accepted the pregnancy," he replied.

"Good. I speak blessings over you in the third month in your mother's womb." I continued month by month speaking blessings over him. He wasn't feeling anything negative, otherwise I would have stopped to do a truth encounter similar to what we did in the second month. If a person was born prematurely I ask the Lord to complete anything that wasn't accomplished due to the early birth. When we got to Sam's ninth month, however, he said he was feeling fearful.

"Do you want to be born?" I asked.

"Not really. I feel safer in here."

"Did you make any inner vows not to live?" I inquired. He wasn't sure about making any inner vows but based on the fruit I saw in his life I led him to break that vow through repentance and renunciation.

"Sam, as an unborn baby in the ninth month in your mother's womb, ask the Lord if He wants you to be born," I instructed.

After a moment of silence Sam indicated that he heard the Lord tell him that He was excited about him being born.

"Are you willing to receive that Sam?"

"Yes, I receive that."

"Okay, then I want to ask you to stand and keep your eyes closed. I pull you through the birth canal." I took his hands in mine and symbolically pulled him out. I had my assistant pull the grave clothes off him. Sam slumped down to the floor sobbing.

"Now as a brand new baby I want you to ask the Lord if He wanted you to be born."

"I see Jesus holding me. He has a big smile on His face," Sam replied weeping with joy.

I have seen many individuals greatly benefitted by using a technique similar to the above scenario. Remember to be sensitive to the Holy Spirit because everyone is different.

It is extremely difficult to minister to yourself, especially in this area of in utero wounds. It usually takes another skilled prayer minister to facilitate healing. However, if possible, you can investigate the circumstances surrounding your conception and your mother's pregnancy. If your mother and/or father are still living, ask them if you were a wanted pregnancy. Inquire about the delivery, the quality of their relationship at the time of conception and throughout the pregnancy, your mother's health and whether the pregnancy placed a strain on the family's finances. Using discretion, talk to aunts and uncles and older siblings who might be able to provide additional information.[ii] Pray that God will heal any in utero wounds.

Prayer

> *Lord, help me know down deep in my heart that I am not a mistake. You planned for me to be born at this time in history. You chose the very egg and the sperm that would join together to form me. Help me know that I am not the cause of my parents' problems. Help me to see my incalculable worth. Lord, put the cross of Christ between me and any negative emotions that I picked up from my mother while I was in her womb. Lord, I forgive my parents for _____ (name any sinful choices such as premarital sex that led to illegitimacy, drug or alcohol use, abandonment of father, attempted abortion, etc.) Lord, wash away by Your Living Water any shame I picked up in the womb. I choose life, in Jesus' name, Amen.*

2

Trauma As a Baby

My mother and father divorced when I was about two years old. Subsequently, I lived with my mother who resided in California and my dad moved all the way to Indiana ostensibly to live near his parents. Because of the 2,000 mile distance I rarely saw my dad until I was old enough to spend an occasional summer with him. Every child longs for his father's nurture and without it a wound festers in the heart. My dad's absence provided fertile ground for the enemy to implant his lies. Later in life I had to deal with the fear of abandonment because I had believed the lie that those that I needed in my life would abandon me, just as my dad abandoned me.

The Principle of Transference

What we believe about our earthly father gets transferred to our Heavenly Father. We commonly refer to this dynamic as the principle of transference. Consequently, I believed the lie that God would not be there for me to protect me—that He would abandon me just like my dad. Keep in mind that theologically, with my mental capacity based on Biblical knowledge, I believed that

God's love for me would never fail. I was familiar with Scriptures such as Romans 8:38-39 which states, *For I am persuaded, that neither death, nor life, nor angels, nor principalities, nor powers, nor things present, nor things to come, nor height, nor depth, nor any other creature, shall be able to separate us from the love of God, which is in Christ Jesus our Lord.*

However, as a small child the enemy whispered in the ear of my heart, "God won't be there for you just like your dad wasn't there for you." And my problem was that I believed him. Down deep in my heart I didn't truly believe that God would always be there for me. When the pressures of life come against us, what we really believe is revealed through our behavior. Peter Lord likes to say, "You practice daily what you really believe, everything else is just religious talk." We can say we trust God but do we actually trust Him? Our English word "believe" comes from an Old English word "bylive." You see, what you truly believe you will live by. I like what Manly Beasley used to say, "You *cannot*, not believe. Either you will believe the truth or you will believe a lie, neutral you cannot be."

No wonder so many Christians have such a tough time truly trusting God. The devil has taken advantage of our father-wounds to inculcate his untruths about God's faithfulness. It is time for us to deal with our lies and ungodly expectations so that we can move on to actually trusting God. Remember the Word is clear that without faith it is impossible to please God.

My father's absence created another problem. It skewed the way I thought about myself. If dad abandoned me then surely something must be wrong with me. In reality, my parent's divorce had nothing to do with me, but the father-wound left my heart vulnerable to receive the valueless lie. I thought that if my dad left me, I must be flawed.

Not long after my mom and dad divorced, my mother started dating another man whom she soon after married. My step-dad was a high-strung individual and the sound of baby's crying sent him into a nervous tirade. If I cried it upset him. His attitude was "children are to be seen and not heard." When my younger siblings were born he would yell at my mother not to check on them or hold them if they were crying. I remember him screaming, "You're going to spoil that child. Let him cry!" What message did that reaction send to us children? It communicated to me that no one will listen. I developed a negative expectation that no one would listen, a subsidiary lie of the valueless spirit. Since I had that expectation I approached all authority figures, including God, with the belief that they would not listen. The funny thing about expectations is that you actually project them on to other people in such a way that it predisposes them to act accordingly.

For example, I heard about a man who was a hard-working, intelligent man, who had the expectation that authority figures would treat him poorly. Sure enough, no matter how well he performed, his employers treated him unfairly. One day at a company meeting, his employer, who intended to recognize him for a job well done, inexplicably began to berate him in the presence of his co-workers. The boss walked away from the meeting shaking his head wondering why he criticized the man when he had intended to compliment him. My theory is that we send out these vibrations that slime the people around us so that they end up acting according to the expectations we place upon them.

It's Safer to be Invisible

Another lie I received as a small child was that it's a lot safer to be invisible. To escape my step father's outbursts of anger I attempted to stay out of his way and be unseen. I purposed to stay quietly in the background. Eventually I developed the expectation that I would be unnoticed. This invisibility may have helped me to elude my step dad's wrath but it played havoc later in life especially with authority figures. I have noticed that as I lead seminars and teach people I have never met that my eyes sort of involuntarily skip over certain individuals in the audience. It's almost as if they are invisible.

A pastor friend of mine told me the story of a man who came up to him after the church service one day and confided in him that he felt invisible because no one noticed him. The pastor listened to his story and tried to console him. Then the pastor invited the man to go out to eat with him and a group from the church. The man accepted the invitation and went with them to the nearby restaurant. Astonishingly, what the man said about his invisibility proved bizarrely true. First, the busboy brought everybody but him some water. Then the waiter went around the table taking everybody's order, but when he got to this man, he skipped right by him as if he wasn't there at all. When this oversight was brought to the waiter's attention he apologized but then later forgot to serve the man his food. When he attempted to get the waiter's attention to bring him coffee the waiter ignored him. Through it all the man remained polite but through the pastor's intervention the request for coffee was heard. Eventually the waiter brought everyone at the table coffee except this man. By this time everyone at the table noticed this weird dynamic and they began apologizing to him for the way he was treated. Then the man said to them, "Oh, don't worry about it. It's no big deal. This type of thing happens to me all the time."

Without having met this individual my guess is that he had developed the expectation that no one would notice him—that he is invisible. His expectation puts out sort of a force field that actually blinds others to his presence. I'm trying hard not to sound weird here but this is the best way I can explain what I have observed. When parents ignore the cries of the infant child the enemy often uses this type of wounding to implant the lie/expectation which states, "no one notices me—I'm invisible. Other common lies/expectations to enter through this wound of neglect are, "I will always have to fend for myself," "I will always be left alone," or "No one cares how I feel."

It's impossible to be a perfect parent. I'm not saying these things to put a guilt trip on parents who are trying their best to raise their children. Sometimes it may be appropriate to let your toddler cry, especially if they are overly tired or are simply throwing a temper tantrum as a form of manipulation or rebellion. Satan can implant his lies even in the healthiest home environments. We live in a fallen world and the very best parents will fall short in some areas. It is important to know that the way the child responds to a circumstance has a greater impact than what actually happened.

For example, three sisters are raised by the same parents, in the same home, in the same environment. Two of them believe that their parents were the greatest and remember a very happy childhood. The youngest sister, on the other hand, is convinced that her parents were cruel and insensitive. Did the parents treat her in another way? Not necessarily so. The third child responded to the shortcoming of her mom and dad differently. She was judgmental of her parents and as an adult needed to repent for her sinful response to them.

The way to overcome the invisibility syndrome is first through recognition. If you identify this dynamic at work in your life repent of any ungodly belief that it's better to be invisible. Repent of the expectation, if applicable, that no one will notice you. Ask God to bring this tendency to death at the cross of Christ. Deal decisively with the valueless spirit with all its lies and subsidiary spirits as delineated in this book. Remember that God's eye is always on you and you are in His thoughts all the time. You are not invisible to Him.

Parent Wanted a Boy/Girl

Deep wounds happen to the heart of the child when their gender is a disappointment to at least one of their parents. When Rosa's mother became pregnant with her, her father was elated but made it clear to all that he wanted a boy. When Rosa's mother gave birth, her father was let down when he saw that she was a female, but within a matter of days he came to terms with his responsibility to be a good father to her. As the days went by he grew to cherish his daughter but she had already been wounded by his words. She received the lie that says, "If I were a male I would be of more value."

This lie was reinforced when her brother was born two years later. Her brother seemed to get all of dad's attention. As his children grew, dad began to spend most of his free time playing with trains and cars with his son. He spent many an evening in the back yard teaching him how to catch and throw a ball. Dad didn't make time to play dollies and tea parties with Rosa or even to hold her on his lap.

Seeking to fill up the void in her life Rosa put aside her desire to play with dolls and other "girlie" things and developed a keen interest in outdoor games. She learned to play baseball and could throw the ball faster, hit the ball farther and run faster than any of the boys her age at school. She begged dad to take her hunting and fishing and took lessons to become an expert archer. She didn't like hanging around other girls her age but much preferred paling around with the boys. Her mother called Rosa her "little tom boy."

Dad's response to Rosa created some gender confusion. In her adult years this lie contributed to her feelings of worthlessness. Through ministry she came to terms with the fact that God created her to be female—that He rejoices in her femininity. She repented for believing the lie that women are of less intrinsic value than men. In such cases I have found it effective to reset the gender polarity. To reset the polarity I simply take both my hands and prophetically grab hold of the invisible spiritual poles of the brain, one at the front of the cranium and one at the back. I reverse the order with a prophetic motion by placing the pole at the back with the one in the front and the one in the front with the one in the back while saying these words, "I reset the male/female polarity of your mind according to kingdom order, in Jesus' Name." This procedure may sound strange but I have witnessed tremendous results using it.

During His earthly ministry Jesus communicated the great value God has placed in women. Many cultures denigrate women making them feel they are of lesser value than men. Mohammed once said that hell was created for women. The Chinese have been known to abort females or to let their girls die because of government sanctions against large families. Even in the United States today women, on the average, get paid less than men for doing the same job, with the same job description, and the same educational and skill-set requirements. But God places equal value in men and women. The Bible says in this regard, *There is neither Jew nor Greek, there is neither slave nor free, there is no male and female, for you are all one in Christ Jesus* (Galatians 3:28, ESV).

Unwise Parental Discipline

Marvin remembers his mother's emotional tirades, He never knew what to expect because the rules changed depending on her moods. He recalls an incident when he was three or four years old. He accidently knocked his bowl of soup off the table and on to the tile floor. His mother, in a fit of rage, boxed his ears and screamed, "You idiot! Can't you just sit at the table and eat your lunch like a normal child? What's wrong with you? Now clean it up and then go to your room. No lunch for you today." He was only four and didn't do it intentionally but mom's discipline didn't fit the situation. At other times his mother reacted to his accidents with perfect patience and calm so poor Marvin didn't know what to expect. He was confused as to how to please mom. Consequently, in his heart he believed that there must be something wrong with him. Unlike Marvin's mom, wise parents apply discipline that fits the misdeed. They are able to distinguish between accidents and defiant disobedience and the rules don't change based on their current frame of mind.

Oftentimes parents over react to their child's misbehavior, bringing shame on the child. Negative words spoken at those times put invisible spiritual labels over the person that affect them the rest of their life. Every time Marvin violated the rules of the house his mother reminded him of past incidences and would shout things like, "You'll never get anything right," or "You're stupid." As an adult he struggled with continually making bad decisions. When he saw that he had, in his heart, believed the lies spoken over him, his prayer minister helped him renounce the lies. He was led to forgive his mother for her contribution in him believing these lies. Then the prayer minister symbolically broke off the invisible placard over him which said, "I can't get anything right, I'm stupid." Today Marvin walks in joyous freedom from the valueless lie.

Prayer

Lord, I forgive _____ (usually mom or dad) for _____ (tell God what they did) what they did was wrong. It wasn't my fault. I let them go free. I repent for the ways I judged them for their behavior. Their behavior was wrong but I judged them as human beings and I repent. I release blessings to them. Please make me a blessing to them. I repent for my anger and for the ways I have judged You God for allowing this to happen in my life. Please bring healing to all of my early childhood memories, in Jesus' name, Amen.

3

The Father Wound

Years ago Heavenly Father instructed me to change the way
I spent my quiet time with Him (at least for a season). He
told me to simply sit and bask in His love. At first I was thoroughly blessed as I meditated on His love for me. But after about
ten or fifteen minutes I began to feel guilty because it seemed so
selfish. I told God that I should be spending my time praying
for others. He didn't say a word. I knew by His silence that He
was waiting for me to be obedient to the last word He gave me.
After about two weeks of spending an hour or so every morning
basking in our Father's love, I had one of those "aha" experiences
as I discovered that by soaking up His love it became easy to
love other people. The end result was that I actually became less
self-centered, probably because I was more secure in the Father's
intimate embrace.

That marked the beginning of the Lord teaching me how important it is for us to experience the Father's love. Many people
have a distorted view of our heavenly Father because they had an
earthly father who didn't accurately model God's love.

What you experienced with your earthly father will greatly affect how you relate to your heavenly Father. Maybe not intellectually, but in our heart we believe that God is like our earthly father. Have you ever wondered why God chose to have us enter this world as helpless babies? I'm convinced that the Lord designed us to begin our lives as infants, totally dependent and vulnerable; because He wants the family to be the setting in which His love is modeled. His plan is that children grow up feeling understood, loved, accepted and nurtured. In this type of environment children grow up with godly self-esteem and a correct view of God. Unfortunately, many homes do not meet this ideal.

Floyd McClung, Jr. points out that there are four types of fathers. The first is the performance-oriented father. The performance-oriented father gives love according to the performance of the child. Love is given or withdrawn in relation to the child's success. Performance demands can take a variety of forms: perhaps it is necessary to pursue a certain career to earn a father's recognition; perhaps a child must conform to a strict family dress code to be accepted. A Christian who has this type of father is often driven into a religious striving.

The second is the passive father. The passive father does not demonstrate love to his child. He does not speak words of love, nor offer any affectionate physical touch of love. One of the principle problems a father's passivity produces in a child is a sense of abandonment leading to the feeling of being alone.

The third is the punitive father. The punitive father gives some form of abusive pain instead of love. This may take place through verbal, physical or sexual abuse leading to fear and distrust of authority.

The fourth is the pretty good father. These fathers generally demonstrate love to the child. No father is perfect but for those who fall in this category, their good effect outweighs the bad. Individuals who had a pretty good father need to move beyond a good relationship with their earthly father and give themselves to their Heavenly Father, trusting fully in Him for their deepest source of love.[iii]

What type of father did you have? This is an important question because our fathers give us our sense of value. I have learned that it is very effective when ministering to people to ask, "When I say the word 'dad,' as a small child what did you feel? Did your father nurture you? Did he tell you he loved you? Did he make you feel loved?" If they had a poor relationship with their dad, I often do an exercise I call "The father's blessing." I tell them that I have a "father anointing" on me and with their permission I would like to stand in and become a surrogate father. I take their hands in mine and look them in the eyes. I ask them to forgive me for not nurturing them, for not telling them I loved them, and for any other failing they previously revealed. Then I illicit a response by asking, "Will you forgive me?" When they answer, "Yes, I forgive you," tears usually come into their eyes. Then I give them a father-hug and speak blessing over them such as, "I'm glad you were born," "I'm glad you are my son/daughter," "I'm proud of you," and "I love you." (I estimate that about 80% of the people coming to me for ministry have never heard their father say I love you.)

At this point the recipient often breaks down weeping, followed by expressions of joy and peace. Emotions flow because there is something in every one of us that cries out for our father's blessing. Remember that our earthly father gives us a sense of value, whether good or bad. The father-blessing exercise not only restores value, it also helps people enter into a more intimate relationship with Father God.

God wants to have more than a superficial relationship with us.

He wants it to be a profound relationship that is heart-to-heart, not merely head-to-head. In God's mind, relationship takes precedence over anything else we do for Him. Like the church in Ephesus (Rev. 2:1-5) we can be constantly busy doing "the Lord's work," but it is not our hard work that pleases Him. What He really wants is that we love Him with all our heart. God is love and the greatest commandment is to love God with every part of our being.

It's not so much doing good things that He is looking for in us, but rather our motives and reasons for doing them. He desires to love and be loved. The most essential objective in the kingdom of God is to establish a deep loving relationship with God, getting to know Him more intimately every day.

True Christianity is about love and intimacy—not merely about having pure doctrine. Though I believe in the absolute necessity of sound doctrine, correct doctrine must not become the primary goal. It is a loving intimate relationship with Almighty God.

I have included in this book a chapter listing Scriptures that will help you understand your intrinsic value. Meditating on these Bible passages will enable you to renew your mind with God's truth about who you are. Scripture memorization/meditation has proven to be the most life-transforming discipline I have incorporated in my life.

The Father-heart of God

A lot of people in our generation have a hard time relating to God as Father. We accepted Jesus. We received the Holy Spirit. But for the most part we ignore the Father. Why is this so? Some churches have presented Father God as harsh. They imply that Jesus is good, loving and kind, but you better watch out for His

Father because the Father represents judgment and wrath.

However, when we come with an open mind to the New Testament we see that Jesus came to reveal the Father; to make known that God is our Father. Jesus' words, His life, His actions reveal to us the heart of the Father. Look at Matthew 11: 28-30 (ESV).

> *"Come to me, all who labor and are heavy laden, and I will give you rest. Take my yoke upon you, and learn from me, for I am gentle and lowly in heart, and you will find rest for your souls. For my yoke is easy, and my burden is light."*

These are well-known, well-loved verses, but look carefully at the context. Back up and look at verses 25-27.

> *At that time Jesus declared, "I thank you, Father, Lord of heaven and earth, that you have hidden these things from the wise and understanding and revealed them to little children; yes, Father, for such was your gracious will. All things have been handed over to me by my Father, and no one knows the Son except the Father, and no one knows the Father except the Son and anyone to whom the Son chooses to reveal him."*

He is not saying what we thought He was saying when He said what He said. Jesus is talking to the Father. Nobody knows the Father except those to whom the Son chooses to reveal Him.

Jesus wants to reveal the Father to all who will come to the Son. The whole context is revealing the Father. How do we have rest? "Take my yoke upon you and learn from me." The backdrop of this saying is revealing the Father. Who was Jesus yoked with? The Father, Jesus yoked up with the Father. Jesus is saying come get yoked up with the Father. A yoke of oxen are tied together and it is amazing how much the Father can carry.

Now check out John 14:6;

> *Jesus said to him, "I am the way, and the truth, and the life. No one comes to the Father except through me."*

The reason Jesus came into the world was to bring us to the Father. Now read John 17:1;

> *When Jesus had spoken these words, he lifted up his eyes to heaven, and said, "Father, the hour has come; glorify your Son that the Son may glorify you."*

Who is Jesus addressing? He is speaking to the Father. Let's read on a few verses in that same chapter.

> *"I have **manifested** your name to the people whom you gave me out of the world. Yours they were, and you gave them to me, and they have kept your word" (v.6, emphasis mine). "I **made known** to them your name, and I will continue to make it known, that the love with which you have loved me may be in them, and I in them" (v. 26, emphasis mine).*

"Manifested" means to reveal, make visible or known what was previously hidden. The word in verse 26 for "made known" means to give thorough knowledge of. What name is He talking about? The context shows it is Father. We need to think about the Hebrew mind-set when it came to names. Names were extremely important. The name they gave their children always seemed to fit the way those children conducted their lives. In pagan culture if you knew the name of a god it gave you a certain degree of power over that deity. But in Hebrew culture the name of God revealed His grandeur and majesty. So the more names of God you knew the more you understood His character.

One common name of God is Elohim. As God came to make covenant with man He revealed Himself with a new name--Yahweh or Jehovah. Yahweh is the covenant name of God. After that God revealed some compound names. He is Elohim to all the people of the world. He is not Yahweh to all people but to those who are in covenant.

Elohim is used over 2,300 times in the Old Testament and Jehovah is used over 6,500 times in the Old Testament. So these names were not hidden. But there is a name Jesus came to reveal that was hidden. Only 14 times in the entire Old Testament is God referred to as Father. Yet, In the Sermon on the Mount alone Jesus referred to God as Father seventeen times! God is referred to as Father 170 times in the New Testament.

Jesus revealed the Father by everything He said. The red letters in your New Testament supposedly represent the words of Jesus but technically they are actually the words of the Father. See what Jesus Himself said;

> *"I tell you the truth, the Son can do nothing by himself; he can do only what he sees his Father doing, because whatever the Father does the Son also does."*
>
> *(John 5:19, NIV)*

> *Jesus answered, "My teaching is not my own. It comes from him who sent me."*
>
> (John 7:16, NIV)

> *So Jesus said, "When you have lifted up the Son of Man, then you will know that I am the one I claim to be and that I do nothing on my own but speak just what the Father has taught me."*

(John 8:28, NIV)

"I and the Father are one."

(John 10:30, NIV)

"For I did not speak of my own accord, but the Father who sent me commanded me what to say and how to say it. I know that his command leads to eternal life. So whatever I say is just what the Father has told me to say."

(John 12:49-50, NIV)

Without a doubt this means that all the kind and tender expressions given to us by Jesus really originated with the Father. They represent the Father's heart.

The well-known parable in Luke chapter 15 teaches us about God the Father.

And he said, "There was a man who had two sons.

And the younger of them said to his father, 'Father, give me the share of property that is coming to me.' And he divided his property between them.

Not many days later, the younger son gathered all he had and took a journey into a far country, and there he squandered his property in reckless living.

And when he had spent everything, a severe famine arose in that country, and he began to be in need.

So he went and hired himself out to one of the citizens of that country, who sent him into his fields to feed pigs.

And he was longing to be fed with the pods that the pigs

ate, and no one gave him anything.

"But when he came to himself, he said, 'How many of my father's hired servants have more than enough bread, but I perish here with hunger!

I will arise and go to my father, and I will say to him, "Father, I have sinned against heaven and before you.

I am no longer worthy to be called your son. Treat me as one of your hired servants.'"

And he arose and came to his father. But while he was still a long way off, his father saw him and felt compassion, and ran and embraced him and kissed him.

And the son said to him, 'Father, I have sinned against heaven and before you. I am no longer worthy to be called your son.'

But the father said to his servants, 'Bring quickly the best robe, and put it on him, and put a ring on his hand, and shoes on his feet.

And bring the fattened calf and kill it, and let us eat and celebrate.

For this my son was dead, and is alive again; he was lost, and is found.' And they began to celebrate.

Now his older son was in the field, and as he came and drew near to the house, he heard music and dancing.

And he called one of the servants and asked what these things meant.

And he said to him, 'Your brother has come, and your father has killed the fattened calf, because he has received him back safe and sound.'

But he was angry and refused to go in. His father came out and entreated him,

but he answered his father, 'Look, these many years I have served you, and I never disobeyed your command, yet you never gave me a young goat, that I might celebrate with my friends.

But when this son of yours came, who has devoured our property with prostitutes, you killed the fattened calf for him!'

And he said to him, 'Son, you are always with me, and all that is mine is yours.

It was fitting to celebrate and be glad, for this your brother was dead, and is alive; he was lost, and is found.'"

(Luke 15:11-32, ESV)

This parable usually has a caption reading "The Parable of the Prodigal Son" and that leads to confusion. The emphasis is not on the son but on the father. "There was a man." The story is about a certain man. He had two sons and neither one understood their father. One son was irresponsible and the other son was religious. The prodigal son came back but the religious son never did grasp the father's heart.

In Jewish culture of the first century it was an unspeakable insult for a son to ask his father for his share of the inheritance because the inheritance was distributed after the father's death. It was tantamount to saying, "Father, I wish you were dead." After receiving his share of the inheritance the son then moves away from home. This was a blatant act of rebellion because in Jewish culture, even after marriage, the sons would continue to live in or near their father's house.

The prodigal used his money to obtain sensual pleasure. How bad was the prodigal's situation? A hog pen for a Jew is about as bad as it can get. As a young man, I too turned my back on my religious upbringing and tried to find love in inappropriate and unfulfilling ways. Like the prodigal I discovered that whatever we lust after, whatever we desire will ultimately control us unless we submit ourselves to the love of the Father. Similar to the prodigal's experience, my lifestyle led to bondage and the bondage eventually brought me to the place of brokenness. God leads us to a place of brokenness so that instead of saying, "Give me. Give me what is mine!" We say "Father, change me. Make me as one of Your hired servants." In our rebellion it is the Father we have left. So He's the One we have to return to in order to be forgiven, healed and restored.

When the prodigal comes to his senses and returns home, his father sees him coming at a distance and runs to meet his son. The father then throws his arms around his son and smothers him with kisses, even though the son is dressed in filthy clothes and smells like pigs. When we come to our heavenly Father that's the way we come—in our sin and shame. Yet He runs to us and hugs and kisses us, showering us with His love. This reality gives me great comfort knowing that I am totally accepted by my Abba Father.

It is amazing that the father in this parable did not wait for an apology to make sure his son was sincere! My heavenly Father is like the father in this story. He does not keep His distance. He does not outline the conditions for me to come back to Him. He runs to me, filled with compassion, and opens wide His arms of love. I don't understand that kind of unconditional love but I'm so glad He does.

All the prodigal says is "I have sinned against heaven and against you. I am no longer worthy to be called your son." He doesn't have to go into all the sordid details. He admits his sin but more importantly, he focuses on the broken relationship. All the father was really interested in was the condition of his son's heart. Likewise, our Father does want us to be repentant, but what He really wants to know is whether or not we love Him and if we are ready to come home.

Grace in reality is a matter of God running to meet our need. Like the prodigal, when we come to the end of our resources, we can go to the throne of God and receive what we need from the Father. What the younger son cannot do in his own ability, the father does for him. This is grace. He gives his son a clean slate, a new beginning. He cancels the debt and then celebrates his son's return. The father gives him the best robe which was a robe of honor worn on festive occasions. He gives him a ring denoting family authority. He gives him sandals for his feet signifying his sonship. Sons wore sandals, servants went barefoot. The father has his servants prepare the very best food for the party. It is remarkable that the father doesn't even tell the servants to give the son a bath before he receives him. He accepts him as he is because he is forgiven. That is grace! The son didn't have to do anything to be loved. The father did it all.

I can identify with the prodigal son because I too was rebellious and tried to find fulfillment in the wrong places. I came to God and by His grace I was wonderfully changed and set free from many bondages of the world.

On the other hand I can relate to the elder brother syndrome. The Lord has revealed some envy and jealousy in my heart. When

I become like the elder brother I am just as desperate for love and attention and self-centered as the prodigal. Normally I just don't see it when I take on the elder brother attitude. Pride keeps me bound. In the Kingdom of God, it is not what I do, but what Christ does in and through me that brings joy to the heart of the Father. My focus must remain on the triune God. When my focus rests on myself, what I have done, what I am doing, I lose my joy. Relationship, not religion, is the key to victorious living. But at the same time, when my heart is right before the Father, then good works and obedience will flow naturally out of love for Him.

Jesus used this parable to demonstrate what the Father is like. Other parables also teach us about the Father's heart. Consider the Parable of the Workers in the Vineyard. This parable tells us the Father is generous and gracious.

"For the kingdom of heaven is like a master of a house who went out early in the morning to hire laborers for his vineyard.

After agreeing with the laborers for a denarius a day, he sent them into his vineyard.

And going out about the third hour he saw others standing idle in the marketplace,

and to them he said, 'You go into the vineyard too, and whatever is right I will give you.'

So they went. Going out again about the sixth hour and the ninth hour, he did the same.

And about the eleventh hour he went out and found others standing. And he said to them, 'Why do you stand here idle all day?'

They said to him, 'Because no one has hired us.' He said to them, 'You go into the vineyard too.'

And when evening came, the owner of the vineyard said to his foreman, 'Call the laborers and pay them their wages, beginning with the last, up to the first.'

And when those hired about the eleventh hour came, each of them received a denarius.

Now when those hired first came, they thought they would receive more, but each of them also received a denarius.

And on receiving it they grumbled at the master of the house,

saying, 'These last worked only one hour, and you have made them equal to us who have borne the burden of the day and the scorching heat.'

But he replied to one of them, 'Friend, I am doing you no wrong. Did you not agree with me for a denarius?

Take what belongs to you and go. I choose to give to this last worker as I give to you.

Am I not allowed to do what I choose with what belongs to me? Or do you begrudge my generosity?'"
(Matthew 20:1-15, ESV)

In like manner the Parable of the Unmerciful Servant in Matthew 18:21-35 teaches us that the Father is forgiving. The Parable of the Persistent Widow in Luke 18 teaches us that God wants to answer prayers speedily.

When we look at Jesus as we read the New Testament, we are seeing an exact representation of God the Father. Jesus Himself said,

> *"If you had known me, you would have known my Father also, From now on you do know him and have seen him."*
>
> *Philip said to him, "Lord, show us the Father, and it is enough for us."*
>
> *Jesus said to him, "Have I been with you so long, and you still do not know me, Philip? Whoever has seen me has seen the Father. How can you say, 'Show us the Father?'*
>
> *Do you not believe that I am in the Father and the Father is in me? The words that I say to you I do not speak on my own authority, but the Father who dwells in me does his works.*
>
> *Believe me that I am in the Father and the Father is in me, or else believe on account of the works themselves."*
>
> (John 14:7-11, ESV)

What do you think about when you think of Jesus? A friend of sinners, moved with compassion, kind, loving, blesses children. Well that is what the Father is like. Remember the story of the woman caught in adultery? Jesus addressed the woman's accusers and said,

> *"Let him who is without sin among you be the first to throw a stone at her." And once more he bent down and wrote on the ground. But when they heard it, they went away one by one, beginning with the older ones, and Jesus was left alone with the woman standing before him. Jesus stood up and said to her, "Woman, where are they? Has*

no one condemned you?" She said, "No one, Lord." And Jesus said, "Neither do I condemn you; go, and from now on sin no more."

(John 8:7b-11, ESV)

We love this passage because Jesus demonstrates His love and grace, but what we see in this story is a picture of the Father. Jesus revealed the grace and compassion of the Father.

If you grew up with a performance oriented, passive or punitive father you may have a hard time relating to God the Father. I want these words to sink into your heart: God the Father is not like your earthly father. He loves you perfectly. Crawl up on His lap and let His arms of love embrace you. There is something about receiving the Father's love that heals our sense of value-lessness.

Journaling

Journaling is the most powerful tool God has used in my life to help me experience the love of the Father. I give credit to Mark and Patti Virkler and their great work of teaching the Body of Christ how to hear God's voice.[iv] Here is a brief overview of the principles of journaling:

1. Still yourself in the presence of God. The expanded version of Psalm 46:10 reads, *"Be still, cease striving, relax, let go, and know that I am God."* Get in a quiet place away from the hustle and bustle of everyday life. Get your body in a relaxed position. (I like to sit in my recliner.) Listening to soft worshipful music can help. Take slow, deep breaths using your diaphragm. For most people being alone out in nature can be very calming.

2. Fix your eyes on Jesus. *Fixing our eyes on Jesus, the author and perfecter of faith, who for the joy set before Him endured the cross, despising the shame, and has sat down at the right hand of the throne of God* (Hebrews 12:2, NAS). Prophetic words flow from the vision that is held before your eyes. Pick out a favorite gospel passage and see Jesus in your mind's eye as you meditate on the story.

3. Tune to the spontaneous flow of thoughts that bubble up in your mind. The Hebrew word for prophecy, *Naba,* literally means to "bubble up."

4. Write down what you hear. *I will climb up to my watchtower and stand at my guardpost. There I will wait to see what the LORD says and how he will answer my complaint. Then the LORD said to me, "Write my answer plainly on tablets, so that a runner can carry the correct message to others."*
(Habakkuk 2:1-2, NLT)[v]

Say to the Lord, "God, I present the eyes of my heart to You. I present the ears of my heart to you." Then write down in your journal, "Father God, what do You want to say to me today about my relationship with You?" Then wait for spontaneous thoughts to alight upon your mind and write down what you sense God is saying. Don't judge the accuracy of the words until after you are done journaling.

Read what you have written down. I recommend that for the first several weeks you present your journaling to another mature Christian you respect to make sure you are hearing correctly. God will not speak to you in a negative, accusatory, caustic way, nor will He say anything that violates His character or the written Word. Until you gain experience, don't use journaling for directive guidance. Instead, use it to develop intimacy in your relationship with Father God.

Prayer

Lord, I present the eyes and ears of my heart to You. I fix my eyes on You Jesus. Lord, what would You like to say to me about my relationship with You? What do You want to say to me about the father-wound?

4

The Mother Wound

B arry, a pastor of a dynamic spirit-filled church, had done everything he knew to do to help his teen-age daughter, Amanda, get the spiritual and emotional freedom she so desperately needed. Barry had an extensive background in deliverance and inner healing, but no matter what he and his wife, Lana, did for Amanda they saw no improvement in her destructive tendencies. They prayed and fasted. They took her to other ministries and counselors, but to no avail. It was only by providential guidance that they discovered the root to their daughter's difficulties.

The source of the problem was traced all the way back to when Lana discovered she was pregnant with Amanda. At that time in their marriage Barry traveled extensively all over the world as an evangelist and conference speaker. They already had three children and Lana wasn't ready to have four she would have to raise virtually by herself. Inwardly she resented the fact that Barry was away from home so much but, at the same time, felt guilty for harboring those feelings because she knew he was doing "the Lord's work." One day, in her third month of pregnancy, she could contain her bitterness no longer and exploded on Barry. She minced no words in expressing her resentment toward the baby in her womb. She also railed on Barry for failing to be home enough to lend a helping hand in rearing the children. That encounter eventually led Barry to back out of most of his commitments as a traveling evangelist and conference speaker. A position opened up for a lead pastoral position at a local church in his area which afforded him the opportunity to spend more quality time with his family.

Even though he made the right choice in changing the direction of his ministry for the sake of the health of his family, extensive damage had been done in the heart of their unborn daughter. The message she received, while still in her mother's womb, was that she was not wanted. Once Barry and Lana realized the source and the depth of Amanda's wounded heart they ministered to her accordingly. Barry repented for his insensitivity and Lana repented to God for her resentment against Barry and Amanda. Then Lana had a heart-to-heart talk with her daughter.

She explained to Amanda the situation regarding her resentment over her pregnancy and then asked her to forgive her for rejecting her in the womb. She held Amanda in her arms and spoke words of blessing. She said, "Amanda, I'm so glad you were born. I am so very proud of you. I'm glad that you are my daughter. I love you, not for what you do but just because you are you." Both mother and daughter had a good cry as they embraced each other. The healing process began and Amanda showed great progress immediately. Until the mother-wound was healed all efforts to help Amanda proved futile.

The lack of nurture we get from our mother deeply traumatizes our spirit. There are two types of trauma—first, bad things that are done to us and second, good things that are withheld. The wounds we receive through neglect are just as damaging, if not more so, than the pain from the abusive things done to us. When

49

our mother failed to hold us when we were afraid, change our diaper when dirty, feed us when hungry, speak words of encouragement, teach us basic hygiene, spend quality time, etc., without a miraculous intervention from the hand of God we will suffer the rest of our lives. The mother-wound typically leads to a breakdown in our relationships with other people, whereas, the father-wound leads to a breakdown in our relationship with God.

At times the mother-wound enters through no fault of our mom. Elizabeth's mother was not supposed to have children because of the severity of her diabetes. When she was born she was premature and assigned to an incubator for six weeks where the medical staff refused to let her mother hold her and feed her. On the other hand, I have ministered to people whose mothers were downright vicious. Stanley's mother, for instance, used to have his older brother hold his hands above his head while she punched him in the stomach over minor infractions. I shudder every time I'm in a line at the grocery store and I hear a mother scream at and berate her child for just being a child. Constant criticism and outbursts of anger create deep wounds.

Thank God He still heals the broken hearted. Jesus said, *The Spirit of the Lord is upon me, because he hath anointed me to preach the gospel to the poor; he hath sent me to heal the broken-hearted, to preach deliverance to the captives, and recovering of sight to the blind, to set at liberty them that are bruised, to preach the acceptable year of the Lord* (Luke 4:18-19, KJV). No mother-wound is beyond the power of Jesus Christ to heal.

The Mother-blessing (Can be adapted to be used as a father-blessing as well)

What can be done to heal the mother-wounds of our hearts? First of all we need to forgive our mother for all of her rejection and lack of nurturing. In my ministry sessions I often have my wife or another female prayer minister stand in and act as a surrogate mother. She asks the person to forgive her for the specific ways she wounded them, eliciting a response. Then she speaks blessings over their life beginning in the womb. Here is an example of a prayer of blessing that the mother or surrogate mother may pray over the person suffering from a mother-wound. Be sensitive to the leading of the Holy Spirit to make sure this is what the Lord wants you to do because not everyone needs, or is ready for this prayer.

Pray this or something like it slowly and from your heart,

> *Lord, I ask that You would bless the egg and the sperm as they were joined together and the cell that was formed by their union. I hold the cross of Christ between the value-less spirit and the baby in the womb and I command the valueless spirit and all its accompanying curses to be destroyed at the cross of Christ.*

> *(Hold their hands and make eye contact.) _____,*
> *I bless the time of your conception. I praise God because of the wonderful way He created you.*

> *Everything God does is marvelous! Nothing about you _____, is hidden from God. You were secretly woven together, but God saw you with His own eyes as your body was being formed.*

> *Even before you were born, God had written in His book everything you would do. God's thoughts toward you are far beyond what you can ever understand and much more than you can ever imagine. If you could count the times God thinks about you they would be more in number than all the granules of sand on the seashores of the world. (adapted from Psalm 139:14-18)*

_____, *I bless your birth process as you came into the world. I thank God for the day you were born. You were well worth all the pain and trouble. I'm so glad you were born.*

God wanted you to be born at this particular time in history and I bless the plans He has for you.

_____, *I bless your infancy. I bless your ability to express yourself through crying. I bless your learning to roll over. I bless your learning to crawl. I bless the first words that came out of your mouth.*

I bless your learning to stand up. I bless your first steps. I bless the time you first began to distinguish between yourself and your exterior world. I bless you for learning how to say "no" and how to say "why".

_____, *I bless you as you grew in wisdom and stature. I bless your learning to read and write. I bless your elementary school age years.*

_____, *I bless your coming into puberty and your transformation from a boy/girl to a man/woman. I bless your individuation process as you learned to be your own person.*

_____, *I bless the day you left home. I bless your family and your career. I bless your children (or future children). May they be mighty in Spirit. I bless the ministry God has given you. I bless your name and your reputation. May the favor of the Lord rest upon you.*

_____, *I'm proud of you. I love you. I'm proud*

*of you, not for what you do, but simply because you are
you. Father God, I ask that You heal _____ of the
mother/father wound. I ask that you give _____
a fresh revelation of your love.*

Conclude with a hug. Hug them until they are finished being
hugged (their body language will let you know). Say repeatedly, "Mommy loves you." Remember that appropriate touch is a
powerful instrument of healing.

The Mother-heart of God

What else can we do to be healed of the mother-wound? We
should act the same way we would if we had a father-wound;
turn to God for healing and bask in His intimate embrace. Most
Christians don't realize that God has both masculine and feminine
characteristics. He is not only a warrior and a conquering king,
He is the nurturing God who tenderly tends to His children. Look
carefully at the creation story recorded in Genesis,

> *Then God said, "Let us make man in our image, after our
> likeness. And let them have dominion over the fish of the
> sea and over the birds of the heavens and over the live-
> stock and over all the earth and over every creeping thing
> that creeps on the earth." So God created man in his own
> image, in the image of God he created him; male and fe-
> male he created them.*
>
> (Genesis 1:26-27, ESV)

God created man in His own image. He created man as male and
female. This means that God is both feminine and masculine. It
takes both the man and the woman to get an accurate view of God.
That's why the first thing the devil tried to do was to separate the
man and the woman so that our view of God would be distorted.

One of the very names of God is El Shaddai. Literally El Shaddai means, "the many-breasted one." God has a breast for every one of His children. In the creation account it says that the Holy Spirit "moved," "hovered" or it could be translated "brooded" over the face of the waters. *The earth was without form and an empty waste, and darkness was upon the face of the very great deep. The Spirit of God was moving (hovering, **brooding**) over the face of the waters* (Genesis 1:2, AMP, emphasis added). Brooding is what a hen does, not a rooster.[vi]

Even though our earthly guardians abandon us, whether purposefully or through no fault of their own, God will never leave our side. Whatever you've been through, God's eyes have always been upon you. Isaiah the prophet said,

> *"Can a woman forget her nursing child, and not have compassion on the son of her womb? Surely they may forget, yet I will not forget you. See, I have inscribed you on the palms of my hands; your walls are continually before Me."*

> (Isaiah 49:15-16, NKJV)

Zephaniah reads,

> *"He is mighty to save, he will take great delight in you, he will quiet you with his love, he will rejoice over you with singing."*
>
> (Zephaniah 3:17, NIV)

The Lord gives us a wonderful picture of His love – that of an infant asleep in the arms of its mother after having been fed at her breast. The baby no longer fusses and squirms, but rests in the mom's gentle embrace. The mother then sings a lullaby and with a deep sense of peace the child sleeps peacefully in her arms.

Another great verse expresses the mother-heart of God. It is found in Psalm 103:13, (NIV), which states, *As a father has compassion on his children, so the Lord has compassion on those who fear him.* The word for compassion in this verse is translated from the Hebrew word *racham*. *Racham* is the Hebrew word used to describe the Father's compassion and tender love for us. It is based on the image of a womb gently embracing a developing fetus, and portrays the intimate embrace of the Father's love. God does not withhold His love for us.

Meditate on the above verses until they get down into the depths of your spirit. Let His tender love fill the void of your heart that cries out for your mother's nurture.

Prayer

Lord, I forgive my mother for the lack of nurture she gave me as a child. I repent for all judgments I made against her. I ask You to come and minister to the mother-wound in my heart and take away the pain. Thank You for your tender compassion that never fails, in Jesus' name, Amen.

5

Abandonment

A s I previously stated, my father and mother divorced when I was still an infant. I lived with my mother on the West Coast while my father moved to Indiana nearly 2,000 miles away. I never saw him again until I was around five years old. I was too young when he left us to have expressed visible sorrow or mourning, yet in my spirit I no doubt sensed his absence and experienced an inner wound. Out of the trauma of divorce the devil planted fear of abandonment in my heart.

The enemy watered that seed every chance he had. When I was five years old I took a train trip with my grandparents from California to New York and back. During a stop at the depot in Chicago I got separated from grandma and grandpa. Imagine the panic of a five year old in a strange place with hundreds of people around me I'd never seen. As I searched for them in the crowded train station the fear of abandonment grew stronger inside me. Thankfully a policeman found me and helped me reunite with my grandparents; nevertheless, more damage had been done. The fear of abandonment can be established in childhood, but it is often not manifested until the person moves out on their own, away from the support of their parents.

The loss of someone you love is a normal part of life. When your loved one dies, moves away, or in some way withholds affection, there are usually feelings of fear that you will be left alone to deal with the complexities of life. Many people suffer from some form of abandonment, whether it is something they are aware of or not. The fear of abandonment creates insecurity and can destroy relationships as it creates a distance between people who love each other.

Many people who suffer from abandonment constantly need to be reassured that they are loved. One spouse will continually ask the other, "Honey, do you really love me?" Ironically, they often break off relationships, not because they don't enjoy the other person, but because they want to be the one rejecting rather than being rejected.

Fear of abandonment opens us up to various diseases including asthma and Hodgkin's disease. Studies have indicated that children of one-parent families are more prone to asthma. We were not created to live in a sustained sense of fear, so fear in any form will eventually take its toll on the body.

My wife Ruthie lost her father when she was age two. He was killed fighting a forest fire and left a wife and four children to fend for themselves. His death wounded Ruthie's little two year old heart and the seed of fear of abandonment was sown by the enemy. For years she suffered from multiple food allergies until she dealt with the fear of abandonment. Once she did the allergies disappeared over night. Praise the Lord!

When Joshua was getting ready to lead the children of Israel into the Promised Land he must have experienced great fear. Otherwise the Lord would not have exhorted him three times in one chapter to, *"Be strong and of good courage"* (Joshua 1:6-7, 9). But God knew that simply commanding Joshua not to fear would not have been enough to help him be courageous. He went on to say, *"I will never leave you nor forsake you"* (Joshua 1:5), and *"the LORD your God is with you wherever you go"* (Joshua 1:9). Just knowing God is right there with us tends to relieve our fears and fill us with courage.

In the Twenty Third Psalm notice the reason David gave for not fearing evil even during the very worst circumstances. *Yea, though I walk through the valley of the shadow of death, I will fear no evil; for **You are with me*** (Psalm 23:4, emphasis mine). No matter what we face God is with us.

One reason He will never abandon us is because He is our Abba Father. Paul said,

> *For you did not receive the spirit of bondage again to fear, but you received the Spirit of adoption by whom we cry out, "Abba, Father." The Spirit Himself bears witness with our spirit that we are children of God.*
> (Romans 8:15-16, NKJV)

The Bible says we are actually born (or born again) into the family of God and God becomes our Abba. Abba means "one who is birthed from his loins."

A friend of mine often makes trips to the Middle East to minister to the churches there. One day while sharing a meal in the home of some locals my friend noticed that some of the children called the father of the home Abba while some of the other children didn't. He asked the father about this and the man answered, "Only the children who are my flesh and blood can call me Abba, the other children living here call me father." In that part of the world Abba means biological father. Abba is also a term of endearment meaning "daddy" or "papa." As a Christian I can confidently say, "God is my daddy." God became my daddy by birth when I was born again into His family.

According to one expert, children go through 4 stages of dealing with their fathers. In stage 1, they call you da-da. In stage 2 they grow and call you daddy. As they mature and reach stage 3 they call you dad. Finally in stage 4 they call you collect.

Actually the word "dad" without further definition doesn't do the word Abba justice. Abba conveys a close intimacy that is reserved for parents and children and obviously not all children enjoy close intimacy with their dad. Jesus' prayer in Gethsemane is the first use of the term in the Scripture (Mark 14:36). The next time (chronologically) it is used is in Galatians 4:6 and then again in Romans 8. It describes a close intimate relationship.

Not only is God our Abba Father but did you know we, as true followers of Christ, are His adopted children? The Greek word for adoption literally means "the placing as a son." It was a legal term used by the Romans in the first century. H.A. Ironside describes the cultural event of adoption: *When a Roman father publicly acknowledged his child as his son and heir, "legally in the forum, this ceremony was called 'the adoption!' All born in his family were children. Only those adopted were recognized [legally] as sons."* (Addition mine).[vii]

Galatians says;

> *Now I say, That the heir, as long as he is a child, differeth nothing from a servant, though he be lord of all; But is under tutors and governors until the time appointed of the father.*
>
> (Galatians 4:1-2 KJV)

In Paul's day the biological child was no different than a servant. He was dressed to look like a servant child; he obeyed rules like a servant child; he was under the rule of another servant. If you were to see all the children of a household, you would not be able to distinguish the cook's child from the master's child. There would be no recognizable difference. All that would change at the time appointed of the father.

At the appointed time the child became a son. There was a ceremony of putting on the toga. It was a predetermined event of the father. The child was a son already, but now he was recognized as such and became a legal heir. When the Bible says I'm adopted it means that all that Christ owns also belongs to me! I'm a joint-heir with Christ. The concept is so stupendous that I can't grasp it with my little peanut brain. It takes the Holy Spirit to make this relationship real in my heart.

I heard a story about a man who had a heart attack and was rushed to the hospital. He could receive little company and was not to be excited. While in the hospital a rich uncle died and left him a million dollars. His family wondered how to break the news to him with the least amount of excitement. It was decided to ask the preacher if he would go and break the news quietly to the man. The preacher went, and gradually led up to the question. The preacher asked the patient what he would do if he inherited a million dollars. He said, "I think I would give half of it to the church." The preacher dropped dead.

If you were told that you were going to inherit a vast sum of money, what would you do? What would you think? How would you react? The fact is that we Christians are sitting on a fortune and acting like paupers. We are joint-heirs with Christ!

Unfortunately, our relationship with our earthly father tends to cloud our vision and impedes our ability to fully enjoy the blessings of our relationship with our heavenly Father. Our earthly fathers may fail and abandon us through death, disease, divorce, or drunkenness, but the good news is that our Father in heaven perfectly and faithfully watches over His children. He will never leave us nor forsake us. He promised it and He cannot lie.

The Orphan Spirit

John's and Rachel's rebellious teenage daughter Rebecca lived her life as if her parents were mean and cruel to her. The truth was that they constantly told her they loved her. They attended every one of her soccer games, established healthy boundaries and tried to spend quality time with her. But no matter how hard they tried to reach out to her, Rebecca remained aloof, responding with a strong will, independence and defiance. Rebecca closed her spirit to her parents' affection and chose to live in isolation from them. She acted as though she did not have a loving and affirming home. She suffered from what is commonly called the orphan spirit.

Many adult Christians experience the inability to feel secure and safe in our Heavenly Father's love. They live their lives as though they have no home—like they don't belong. They feel abandoned by God. They constantly struggle with feeling that they are not totally accepted and favored by God. They have the orphan spirit.

Through personal ministry, John and Rachel discovered that the orphan spirit took hold of Rebecca as a small child. In the early years of their marriage John often responded harshly to his wife and daughter. Emotionally he was "shut down" except for his frequent outbursts of anger.

The Lord revealed a particular incident that occurred when Rebecca was about five years old that seemed to close her spirit to her dad. It happened one day when John came home from a hard day at the office. Rebecca had been waiting excitedly for her daddy to come home so she could show him the new shoes momma bought her that day. When she approached her dad as he entered the front door, rather than rejoicing with her, he impatiently told her to go outside and play. That wounded her spirit and she lost the desire to trust him with her emotions.

Feelings of being a spiritual orphan were cultivated time and time again through John's harsh, authoritarian, demanding behavior. By the time Rebecca was ten, however, John experienced a life transforming encounter with Jesus Christ. Through personal ministry he received healing from deep wounds from his childhood. The dramatic change in him was evident to all—all that is except Rebecca. The orphan spirit kept her from seeing the good in her father and she continued to judge his motives as she closed herself off from his love.

The orphan spirit can ruin your relationships with God, family members, and others. Here are some indicators to help you identify the orphan spirit in your life or the life of your child:

1. They focus on the faults of their parents.

2. They fail to understand that their parent's hurtful attitudes and actions came as a result of their own unhealed issues and pain. As a result of their pain and judgments they live in a state of discouragement, disappointment and rejection.

3. They have lost basic trust in parental authority. They have lost the ability to hold their heart open to others because they judge their motives to be impure.

4. They have an inability to open their heart to be close, vul-

nerable and honest in relationships.

5. They close their spirit to their parents in time of need.

6. They have an independent spirit. In their heart they say, "God, I can't trust You to help me so I would rather handle everything myself."

7. They control their relationships with anger, passivity or isolation. An example of isolation is to become absorbed in watching the news, sports, or weather on TV.

8. Their relationships become superficial because they fear opening their hearts lest they be hurt again. They keep their distance from those in authority or from those who may be able to provide the help they need.

9. They feel they have no one to trust to affirm and admonish them.

10. They feel they have no place to belong and be protected.

11. They begin to find comfort and identity in counterfeit affections such as addictions to alcohol, drugs, food, gambling and pornography. They find security in money or position.

12. They find it easy to see the faults in others and use that as an excuse to not get close to them. They have a hard time maintaining an intimate love relationship with God. Their Christian experience is based on keeping the rules rather than knowing God.[viii]

Jack Frost said, "The root of feeling like a spiritual orphan is one of the greatest hindrances to people receiving their healing and walking in expressed love, intimacy, and in healthy relationships. It takes basic trust being restored in order to daily feel secure enough to receive the love that is needed to heal our wounded hearts.

The more love and comfort we are able to receive, the less fearful we are of opening our hearts to intimate, loving relationships. We must be willing to let go of our need to suppress our childhood pain and to control our emotions in order to open our hearts to receive the Father's healing love and to walk in true intimacy with others."[ix]

Prayer for Healing the Orphan Spirit

Father, I recognize that I have an orphan spirit. I bring my past and present hurts of feeling abandonment to you for healing. Jesus, I ask that you stand with me in these hurts and I reach out to you for full restoration. I forgive those who have walked away from me. Lord, I ask that you forgive me for my anger, bitterness, blame or other feelings against others or myself. I forgive myself. I set others free from my expectations that they might abandon me some day. Holy Spirit, I ask that You guide my friendships and relationships. Help me to reach out in friendship to others and to trust You, Lord, in that relationship.[x]

6

Rejection

R ejection represents one of the most destructive forces facing mankind. Rejection keeps you from reaching your destiny by tying you to your past. The spirit of rejection acts as a magnet. It likes to draw rejection to itself. That's one reason why you know people who keep getting rejected over and over. Herein lies the answer to why people who suffer deep rejection in their first marriage turn right around and go into another relationship filled with rejection.

John, a sixty-one year old pastor knows what rejection feels like because he experienced it at an early age. His mother and father divorced when he was yet an infant and his father moved several thousand miles away. This was his mother's second marriage to fail. Shortly thereafter his mother remarried for the third time. His stepfather was loud, angry, and explosive and he feared his venomous tirades.

As a young boy growing up he received little to no nurture from him. For instance, he recalls wanting to learn to play catch with a baseball and glove. With some coaxing he finally talked his step dad into going in the back yard to play ball. The step dad had him stand in front of the cinder block wall and proceeded to burn it in. The hard ball hurt John's hand even through the glove and so he started jumping to the side when he threw his fastball. That only infuriated the step dad and he began to call John a sissy. His favorite term was "panty-waist" and John determined from that point on to avoid contact with him if possible.

Neither John nor his siblings ever heard him say that he loved them. Later, after the kids were grown, his step dad changed and never forgot to tell the adult children he loved them every time they visited their parents, and for that John is grateful. But the damage had already been done.

Another factor that deepened the rejection was that his mother had children from each of her three marriages. His two older sisters' last name was Johnson, his three younger siblings were Merriman's and he was the one only with his last name. It always hurt when friends would ask him why his name was different. Keep in mind that when he grew up in the 1950's rarely did you see couples get divorced, remarried, and living in blended families.

He also felt like he didn't get his parents approval unless he performed. If he brought home a report card with all A's and B's his parents never gave him praise for doing a good job. Instead he heard them say, "Next time bring home all As." A performance-based home breeds rejection and fear of rejection.

To make matters worse, his stepfather did not make a lot of money as a construction worker and it proved difficult to feed and clothe a family of eight. Consequently, the children often attended school dressed in raggedy hand-me-downs and shoes with holes or flapping soles. Needless to say, John received a lot of ridicule from his classmates which added to the overall feeling of rejection.

Rejection devalues people and strikes a devastating blow to one's sense of value. The noun "rejection" comes from the verb "to reject." Webster's Dictionary defines "reject" as "to refuse to take, to discard or throw out as worthless, useless, or substandard; cast off or out; to pass over or skip; to deny acceptance, care, love, etc." We have all received rejection from one degree to another and none of us likes it.

If your school classmates ever called you names you have experienced rejection. If you have ever been picked last when they were choosing teams you know rejection. If you have ever been ignored, persecuted, maligned, made fun of, betrayed, abandoned, abused, forgotten, or overlooked, then you know what rejection is about. Of course some acts of rejection hurt more deeply than others.

I have discovered that part and parcel with the spirit of rejection is the distorter spirit. The distorter spirit twists the words of another person so that what you hear them say is completely different than what they actually said. One man jokingly said, "I know that you believe you understand what you think I said, but I'm not sure you realize that what you heard is not what I meant."[xi]

When a person has the spirit of rejection they tend to twist and misinterpret what other people say and do. For example, a husband comes home from work and he says to his stay-at-home wife, "Honey, what did you do today?" Rejection in her will hear him say, "You lazy thing, why didn't you do something more constructive with your time?" A husband says to his wife, "Honey, I really like your new hairdo." She hears him say, "Why did you get your hair styled that way? It looks ridiculous on you."

Or your pastor walks right by you at church without acknowledging your presence. The truth may be that he is in a hurry to get something ready before the service starts but you interpret it to mean that you're not appreciated and it might be a good idea to start looking for another church. Rejection causes a person to be easily offended so other people have to watch what they say around them.

Bible Meditation on Rejection

I encourage you to do a Bible meditation on rejection. Using a Bible concordance, look up all the passages that relate to the subject and read them carefully. Ask the Lord to speak His truth regarding each verse and record what He tells you. Remember that the rejection you received in your life may open the door to the valueless spirit. As an example, here is a list of declarations that are based on a Biblical meditation I did. You will probably find other truths regarding rejection that can be made into faith declarations. Make these declarations every day for thirty days:

The rejection I receive may lead to my promotion.

Jesus said to them, "Have you never read in the Scriptures: 'The stone the builders rejected has become the capstone; the Lord has done this, and it is marvelous in our eyes?'"

(Matthew 21:42 NIV)

It was God's plan for Jesus to be rejected. God uses my rejection for His purposes.

He then began to teach them that the Son of Man must suffer many things and be rejected by the elders, chief priests and teachers of the law, and that he must be killed and after three days rise again.

(Mark 8:31 NIV)

I will not be surprised if I am rejected.

Jesus was rejected. John 1:10-11. Throughout His ministry He received rejection. He was rejected at Nazareth: Luke 4:16-30. He was rejected by his own family: Mark 3:21. He was rejected by the teachers of the Law: Mark 3:22 – they said He was demon possessed. He was rejected at the cross: Mark 8:31. *The servant is not greater than his lord. If they persecuted me, they will also persecute you* (Jn. 15:20, KJV). *Yea, all of you who will live godly in Christ Jesus will suffer persecution* (2 Tim. 3:12, KJV).

He was rejected but He wasn't embittered by it. I will not be embittered by rejection.

Then said Jesus, Father, forgive them; for they know not what they do.
(Luke 23:34 KJV)

If I am rejected by men I am accepted by God.

Can a woman forget her suckling child, that she should not have compassion on the son of her womb? Yea, they may forget, yet will I not forget thee. Behold, I have graven thee upon the palms of my hands; thy walls are continually before me.
(Isaiah 49:15-16, KJV)

God thinks about me all the time. He does not neglect me or reject me.

I will praise thee: for I am fearfully and wonderfully made: marvelous are thy works; and that my soul knoweth right well. My substance was not hid from thee, when I was

*made in secret, and curiously wrought in the lowest parts
of the earth. Thine eyes did see my substance, yet being
unperfect; and in thy book all my members were written,
which in continuance were fashioned, when as yet there
was none of them. How precious also are thy thoughts
unto me, O God! How great is the sum of them! If I should
count them, they are more in number than the sand: when
I awake, I am still with thee.*

(Psalm 139: 14-18, KJV)

I am valuable to God.

*And fear not them which kill the body. But are not able to
kill the soul: but rather fear him which is able to destroy
both soul and body in hell. Are not two sparrows sold for
a farthing? And one of them shall not fall on the ground
without your Father. But the very hairs of your head are
all numbered. Fear ye not therefore, ye are of more value
than many sparrows.*

(Matthew 10:28-31, KJV)

God chose me.

*Ye have not chosen me, but I have chosen you, and or-
dained you, that ye should go and bring forth fruit, and
that your fruit should remain: that whatsoever ye shall ask
of the Father in my name, he may give it you.*

(John 15:16, KJV)

*According as he hath chosen us in him before the foun-
dation of the world, that we should be holy and without
blame before him in love: Having predestinated us unto
the adoption of children by Jesus Christ to himself, according to the good pleasure of his will. To the praise of*

the glory of his grace, wherein, he hath made us accepted in the beloved.

(Ephesians 1:4-6, KJV)

I am His child.

For ye have not received the spirit of bondage again to fear; but ye have received the Spirit of adoption, whereby we cry, Abba, Father.

(Romans 8:15, KJV)

I am loved by God.

For I know the thoughts that I think toward you, saith the LORD, thoughts of peace, and not of evil, to give you an expected end.

(Jeremiah 29:11, KJV)

For God so loved the world, that he gave his only begotten Son, that whosoever believeth in him should not perish, but have everlasting life.

(John 3:16, KJV)

Faith Decree

God uses rejection to cause my growth and move me into spiritual realms I probably would not have gone had I not experienced the rejection. He uses rejection to purify my life and to propel me to higher heights in the Spirit. I decree that God has set me free from the stronghold of rejection.

Freedom from Rejection

Here are some exercises that can be done along with inner healing and deliverance methods delineated in this book.

First, make a list of the ways you have been rejected by others and the ways you have rejected others. Write their names in the following form along with a key word to describe the rejection event. Then ask the Holy Spirit what He wants to say to you about each situation, and write that in the adjacent column. Make sure to forgive from your heart every person who rejected you.

How do you forgive from the heart and not just the head? It is through using the language of the heart. The language of the heart is that of flowing thoughts and flowing pictures.

Go back to the memory of the time when you were rejected. See the person you are forgiving in your mind's eye. See yourself at the age and in the scene where the offense occurred. See the offense and yourself in the scene where it happened, and at the age it happened.

From that vantage point say to the one who hurt you, "I forgive you. I let you go free. I lay nothing to your charge. I require nothing of you. I release blessings to you."

Rejection Events and People	The Holy Spirit's Truth

Prayer to Overcome Rejection

In the name of Jesus, I confess and repent for coming into agreement with the spirit of rejection. I repent and renounce the rejection I have received from_____ (person).

I ask you, Lord Jesus, to forgive me. I forgive myself, from my heart, for this rejection, and I release myself from any guilt or shame from this rejection. In the name of Jesus, and by the power of His blood, I cancel Satan's authority over me in this rejection of _____(name specific area mentioned above).

Lord Jesus, I invite you into my heart to heal me of this rejection. Holy Spirit, what do You want to say to me about this situation.

Write on the previous form what the Holy Spirit says to you. You may need to use extra paper.

7

The Victim Spirit

I define the "victim mentality" and the "victim spirit" somewhat differently. Persons with the victim mentality blame everyone else for the negative things that happen to them. They make poor choices and then accuse others for causing their predicament.

Arnold didn't get the promotion he so desperately desired. When his wife asked him why he thought he didn't get the new position he explained that Melissa (his supervisor) didn't like him—that she was out to get him because she doesn't like men. However, Arnold forgot the fact that Melissa had warned him three different times for making excessive personal phone calls. He also didn't mention that he had been written up for spending company time surfing the web.

Arnold has a victim mentality. Another example of the victim mentality is that in American society we see a growing number of individuals relying on government to fix their problems. This mind-set keeps them from taking the initiative to better themselves. But the *victim mentality* is dissimilar to *victim spirit*.

Those who suffer from a victim spirit don't necessarily do anything wrong to attract negative circumstances nor do they automatically blame others for their bad set of circumstances. They may in fact diligently make responsible choices and meticulously follow sound principles for successful living. While everyone suffers from injustices, those with a victim spirit suffer inordinately more than others. It is as if misfortune is attracted to them like a magnet. As destructive situations reoccur, the person believes that the future only holds bad things for them—that there is nothing that can be done to change the pattern of repeated "bad luck." Eventually they conclude that it is all their fault—that something is wrong with them.

When I was a kid we sometimes played the mischievous game called "kick me." This game entailed making a sign on a piece of notebook paper which read "kick me." Then at school recess we would secretively tape it to the back of one of our playmates. Other students walking by would playfully kick our friend in the derriere making him wonder why everyone was kicking him. That game only works on someone once because they catch on quickly that there must be a sign taped to their back.

With regard to the victim spirit, however, they find themselves being kicked over and over again. It is as if there is an invisible "kick me" sign taped to the back. I call it a victim placard. I believe it is a literal sign in the spirit world over a person's head which signals oppressor spirits to stir up others to treat them unfairly. The oppressor spirit thrives on and is drawn to the victim spirit. At times, when ministering to an individual, I have been led by the Spirit of the Lord to prophetically tear down the victim placard over their head and give it to the Lord for His disposal. It may sound weird but when I do this exercise, as led by the Holy Spirit, the person usually senses a noticeable "shift" in their spirit and increased freedom.

Possible Entry points

Mary married George who had a good job at the time of their marriage. Within six months he quit his job and began heavy drinking on a daily basis even though he didn't have an alcohol addiction prior to their wedding. He wouldn't lift a finger to help her around the house and he refused to look for employment. He didn't care about her feelings and after two years she saw no hope of change and filed for divorce.

Within a year she met Joe. As the attraction between the two grew, Mary didn't want to repeat the mistake of her first marriage. The factors that assured her about him were that Joe had always been an avid teetotaler, and that he had held a steady good-paying job with the same company for eight years. This time, however, much to Mary's utter shock and dismay, within four months of marriage Joe quit his job. Even though he wasn't a drinker, he began to tipple. Eight months later he was paying daily visits to a nearby pub where he drank himself into oblivion. Coming home from one such visit he was arrested for DUI. He, like George, refused to find another job but at least he had a good excuse. Because his driver's license had been rescinded he didn't want to suffer the embarrassment of relying on public transportation to get to work.

Mary was at her wits end. In desperation she sought a Christian counselor to get some direction and to deal with the issues in her life. As she told him her story she revealed her childhood trauma of living with an alcoholic father. One of her most hurtful memories was when mom and dad had planned on taking her to Disney World. The excitement grew as they planned the trip. She stayed awake most of the night before they were to leave on vacation because she couldn't stop thinking about the exciting rides and fun things they would do in Orlando. She was out of bed by 6:00 AM and ready to help pack the car and leave. However, mom came into her room and with tears in her eyes explained to Mary that dad went out drinking the previous evening and hadn't been home all night. He started another one of his drinking binges and they would have to postpone their trip to Disney World.

This experience not only broke Mary's heart, it opened her up to receive the lie that men can't be trusted. Not only did she make the inner vow that she would never marry an alcoholic like her dad, she also received the expectation that, "I will choose men who are irresponsible, men who disappoint me." In such cases a wife can actually "slime" her husband, which puts a spiritual pressure on him to do things which are totally out of character for him.

Carl's mother didn't properly care for him when he was sick as a child. One day when he was about six years old he felt sick and went to bed. Suddenly he felt something erupting in his stomach. He scrambled out of bed to make a mad dash for the bathroom but he couldn't make it before vomiting all over the floor. He called for his mother for comfort, but when she saw the mess she made him clean it up, even though he was very ill. What was the ungodly belief Carl received through this experience? He believed that, "I have to take care of myself because no one else will." Think of the harm that belief caused in his trust relationship with God and family members.

Kathy tried to tell her parents that her brother had molested her. They told her she was being overly dramatic and didn't believe her. What lie did she receive at that point? She believed the lie that says, "My feelings/thoughts don't count so I'll keep them to myself."

Jill's step father molested her. The lie she received was, "I'm bad/ dirty" and the expectation that developed within her was, "I will attract people who hurt me or control me."

When Joan was a teenager she snooped through some of her father's paperwork in his home office. She ran across a love letter from a woman with whom he was having an affair. Apparently, her mother knew nothing about the affair. Joan's heart was crushed with the pain of betrayal and the lie she received was, "Women are doormats."

Bill's mom was often angry and moody. Through this dynamic he was invalidated and received the ungodly belief that, "It's not safe to express myself."

There are an endless number of scenarios to illustrate how these lies gain entry and build within the individual the victim spirit. Ask the Lord to bring to your memory any traumatic experience from your past that He wants to heal. Then ask Him to reveal to you any lie or negative expectation that you received as a result of the trauma.

Recognition is the Key to Healing

Here are some questions to ask yourself to help you determine whether or not you operate under a victim spirit;

1. Do you have a history of broken relationships? (Mean things are said, you or your partner say or do hurtful actions?
2. Do you experience recurring hurt in relationships where fractious words are said and hurtful things are done?
3. As a child do you remember yelling at your parents?
4. As a child do you remember your parents yelling at you?
5. Is there any sexual abuse or sexual promiscuity in your background?
6. As a child do you remember sensing that your opinions were invalidated?
7. As a child did you have any life-threatening experiences?

(cord around your neck at birth, parents didn't want the pregnancy, mom was very sick as a result of her pregnancy, near drowning experience, accidents involving fire, etc.).

8. As a child did you experience rejection and abandonment? (Parent or loved one leaves through divorce or death.)

9. Do you often have intense feelings of anger and/or hopelessness?

10. Do you often blame yourself or others for your bad set of circumstances?

11. Do you experience more "bad luck" than most people you know?

12. As a child did you feel betrayed by adults who were supposed to love, nurture and protect you?

If you answered yes to one or more of these questions than you are probably operating under a victim spirit. The victim spirit is an underling of the valueless spirit but it is very powerful and destructive in and of itself. Beloved, if you recognize the victim spirit at work in your life don't give in to it. Don't let people who are driven by the oppressor spirit control you.

Through my research the best resource I have found on the subject is Plumbline Ministries. Arthur Burk has written an excellent article entitled, *Overcoming the Victim Spirit,* and can be obtained free online. I like what Arthur Burk says, "The most obvious sign of a victim spirit mind-set is that the victim can explain away why it is right for things to be wrong, and more specifically, why it is right for them to stay in a situation where they are consistently mistreated."

The good news of Christ is that you don't have to stay a victim. God has given us the authority to take dominion *over* our circumstances so that we don't have to remain *under* our circumstances. I encourage you to repent for having come into agreement with the victim spirit. Ask God to bring the victim mind-set to death at the cross and bring all you thoughts into submission to Christ.

Prayer

Lord, I repent for having come into agreement with the victim spirit. I ask You to bring this structure in my life to death at the cross of Christ. I command the victim spirit to leave me now, in Jesus' name. I decree and declare that the victim placard is removed from me. By God's grace I will no longer be a victim but will live in Christ's victory (Remember to enlist the help of an experienced prayer minister to command the victim spirit to leave and to pull off the victim placard.), in Jesus' name, Amen.

8

Isolation

Jim couldn't seem to connect. His wife Sarah thrived on meeting new people and building relationships. She desired for her and Jim to be plugged into the same church but whatever church they attended Jim never made the effort to make friends. He seemed to always have a legitimate reason for not participating in most of the church functions. Either he had to work late, had a headache, or didn't want to miss an important ball game on TV. Having been raised in a Christian home he believed in Christ. He faithfully attended Sunday morning worship but never wanted to hang around after the service for fellowship. He had his fishing and golf buddies but Sarah was his only real Christian friend.

Why does Jim isolate himself from fellow Christians? God never intended for us to live in isolation. He planned for us to be connected and inter-dependent on one another. When we give our hearts to Christ through the new birth experience the Holy Spirit unites us together with other believers and we as individuals become part of the Body of Christ. If God is not the author of isolation guess who is? God puts us together in one body so that we can gain strength and encouragement from one another.

Carroll Thompson, retired professor at Christ For the Nations Institute, has strong words to say about the problem of isolation. "Isolation is the number-one problem in this society. The breakdown of the family and the lack of brotherhood in the community has left a generation living in a vacuum of emotional needs. Without union, without bonding, they live in emptiness and spaciousness. Without purpose and meaning in life, they live for the moment, hoping to experience something that will make life worthwhile."[xii]

George Gallup once told a group of church leaders "Americans are perhaps the loneliest people on earth today." He suggests that Americans suffer from "personal isolationism." Isolation and the resulting loneliness take a serious toll on our well-being, both socially and spiritually. Much of it begins with the lie that states, "I'm of no value" or more specifically, "I'm not significant," which is followed by feelings of hostility, anger, and depression.

There are numerous reasons why individuals choose to detach themselves. Perhaps they have been hurt by Christian friends who have betrayed them and they decide not to open their heart enough to be hurt again. Because of their woundedness they have a hard time trusting "church people." It could be that as a child their best friend moved away leaving a gaping wound in their heart and they made an inner vow that they would never get close to anyone again. From that experience they may have developed a fear of loss of relationships.

In Jim's case, however, his isolation was tied to his sense of lack of value. He didn't think he had much to contribute and felt that other believers were far more spiritually advanced than he. Sarah proved that perception. She participated in two day-time ladies Bible studies every week, attended Christian growth seminars about once a month, prayed for hours every day and was considered the resident theologian of their home. How could he compete with that?

Jim's mother was a deeply spiritual woman who was determined to raise up her children in the ways of the Lord. She put her offspring on a strict regimen of Scripture memorization and every week they had to recite five assigned verses from memory. Jim, the youngest of three, tried his best to keep up with his older siblings but often fell short. His perfectionist mom insisted that they make no mistakes as they quoted from the King James Version. Sometimes when quoting a passage, which was familiar to his siblings, they would criticize and laugh at him for his mistakes. On one such occasion he received the lies from the enemy, "Something is wrong with me. I'm not as spiritual as other people. If I isolate myself from other Christians I won't get hurt." Throughout his life, in the choices he made, you can see how this lie was played out over and over again.

Suzette, on the other hand, likes to mingle with people after church. She attends various functions throughout the week and knows a good number of people by name. But she has no real "soul friends." On the outside she appears to be a friendly person but on the inside the loneliness at times is almost unbearable to her. What is her problem? As a small child she received the lie that she is of no intrinsic value. The subsidiary lie in her life was, "If I let others know the real me they will reject me." She believed there was something inherently wrong with her—something unredeemable. Consequently, she put up a wall around her heart to protect herself from the fear of being found out.

Years ago I recognized this tendency in me. I didn't want people to know the real me because I feared that they would think less of me. I feared their judgment. But as I opened up and shared my heart I found the exact opposite to be true. The more transparent I became the more others identified with me and felt safe to share their struggles.

The truth is that we are all wicked and corrupt to the core of our being. *The heart is deceitful above all things and desperately sick; who can understand it* (Jeremiah 17:9, ESV)? It is only by the mercy and saving love of God that He makes our hearts brand new. Even as Christians, parts of our heart need cleansing.

> *Since we have these promises, beloved, let us cleanse our-selves from every defilement of body and spirit, bringing holiness to completion in the fear of God.*
>
> (2 Cor. 7:1, ESV)

Judgments

This brings me to the subject of judgments. It's time that we in the Body of Christ stop judging one another. No wonder we iso-late ourselves and fail to bond with one another. We all hate to be judged. Yes, it is true that I can make a judgment as to whether or not a particular action is right or wrong. But I sin when I begin to judge a person's motive or worth. When I sense that a fellow Christian will not judge me it is like a breath of fresh air. It's a blessing to know I am free to be myself when I'm around him. We need to feel safe before we can develop close relationships.

Jesus said,

> *"Judge not, that you be not judged. For with what judg-ment you judge, you will be judged; and with the same measure you use, it will be measured back to you."*
>
> (Matthew 7:1-2, NKJV)

If you judge others you will attract people's judgments toward yourself like a magnet.

The apostle Paul said,

> *Therefore you are inexcusable, O man, whoever you are who judge, for in whatever you judge another you condemn yourself; for you who judge practice the same things.*
>
> (Romans 2:1, NKJV)

Ironically, if you judge others for being judgmental you will end up doing the same thing.

> *Who are you to judge another's servant? To his own master he stands or falls...*
>
> (Romans 14:4, NKJV)

Scripture is very clear that we are not to be judgmental and critical. If you do not turn from this evil it will be difficult for you to live in corporateness.

There is a law in physics that states that for every action there is a corresponding equal and opposite reaction. To illustrate, when I used to practice on my own for a tennis match, I would hit the ball against a high concrete wall. It came right back at me. I hit it again harder and the ball returned with increased velocity and it did this every time giving me a good workout. And so it is with our judgments. They return to us every time without fail.

If you believed any of these lies presented in this book it means you have judged somebody—mom, dad, authority figures, God or even yourself. I have discovered that judgments and the valueless lies are inextricably intertwined.

The Good Soul Tie Inhibitor spirit

I have discovered that there exists a whole genre of evil spirits connected to the valueless strongman. That is because their mission is to make our lives miserable so that we cannot walk in our God-given destiny. One such spirit is the good soul tie inhibitor spirit. Let me explain.

A good soul tie is developed when we make a spirit to spirit connection with another human being in a godly fashion. David and Jonathan enjoyed such a close relationship that it is said that they had a good soul tie.

> *And it came to pass, when he had made an end of speaking unto Saul, that the soul of **Jonathan** was knit with the soul of David, and **Jonathan** loved him as his own soul.*
> (1 Samuel 18:1 KJV)

A soul tie is actually a spirit to spirit bonding with another human being. I have a good soul tie with my wife and I can often sense what she is feeling without her even saying a word.

But there is an evil spirit whose role is to block the development of good soul ties making it difficult to bond with others in healthy relationships. God desires that we be knit together with others in the Body of Christ . . .*that their hearts may be encouraged, being knit together in love, to reach all the riches of full assurance of understanding and the knowledge of God's mystery, which is Christ,* (Col. 2:2, ESV).

If you sense that the good soul tie inhibitor spirit is present address it like this, "Listen to me you good soul tie inhibitor spirit. I reject you, I renounce you, and I break all agreements with you. I bind and break your power. I cancel your assignments and cast you out now, in Jesus' Name."

Here is an exercise a husband and wife may do to strengthen the spirit to spirit bonding between them. (This is only meant for married couples.) Take all your clothes off from the waist up including under garments so that you are touching skin-to-skin.[xiii] Then hold each other with no expectation that this intimate embrace will lead to sex. This exercise is not about sex per se, but about connecting with your mate's spirit. The human spirit resides in the stomach/chest area and there is a portal to the spirit in the region somewhere around the sternum. Chest-to-chest, hold each other, opening your heart to your spouse. Let your spirit feel his/her spirit. Then ask God to bond your spirits together. Take your time not rushing through this exercise. Do this exercise daily for ten or fifteen minutes over the period of a few weeks, until you sense your spirits bonding together.

Prayer

Lord, I repent for the ways I have judged those around me. I confess that I judged _____(name the persons). I surrender my right to have an opinion about the motives of other people. I repent for the ways I have lived in isolation. You didn't create me to be an island but to live connected to others. Help me to stay connected to others especially to my immediate family and to the Body of Christ.

9

Pride and Self-centeredness

One of the big problems a valueless sufferer experiences is that their life becomes self-focused. Their thoughts center on themselves to compensate for their sense of worthlessness and to hide their flaws from others. Pride and self-centeredness are two sides of the same coin. The pride side relates to the demonic or spirit, while the selfishness side comes from what the Apostle Paul calls the "flesh."

You can't cast out the flesh. It must be brought to the cross of Christ and crucified on a daily basis. Once we allow the flesh to rise up, we open the door for the enemy to rebuild the stronghold of pride. Both pride and self-centeredness often flow from the valueless spirit, though not necessarily so.

Pride and self-centeredness open the door to a whole host of problems. For example, the Bible says,

Likewise you younger people, submit yourselves to your elders. Yes, all of you be submissive to one another, and be clothed with humility, for "God resists the proud, but

gives grace to the humble." Therefore humble yourselves under the mighty hand of God, that He may exalt you in due time,

(1Peter 5:5-6, NKJV)

I don't know about you but I don't want God to resist me. Maybe this is one reason valueless sufferers always seem to struggle in life.

People with the valueless spirit usually struggle to find God's direction for their lives. Do you want to clearly hear God's voice? Are you seeking His guidance but He seems far away? Many times during my Christian walk I needed some direction in a matter and received no clear answer. Finally, out of frustration and anger, I would cry out to God, "Lord just tell me. Make it clear and I'll do whatever you tell me. Just speak to me!" Can you relate?

What represents one of the main obstacles in getting clear direction from God? According to Psalm 25:9, the answer is pride. *He guides the humble in what is right and teaches them his way (Psalm 25:9, NIV).* Pride becomes a huge block in our spiritual ears. A humble person tunes his ears to hear the voice of God and maintains a teachable heart.

As a kid I had a pony named Duke. Every time I rode Duke he gave me trouble. He tried his best to buck me off. He went where he wanted to go including running under low tree branches to make me fall. And when that didn't work he tried to scrape my legs against barbed wire fences and then reach around to bite me. He stubbornly resisted any attempt to train him. Duke was just plain ornery to the bone.

The reason I couldn't guide him was because he possessed a mind of his own. One of the chief characteristics of pride is self-exertion and when I exert self I have a hard time letting God guide me. King David, inspired by the Holy Spirit, put it this way,

I will instruct you and teach you in the way you should go; I will counsel you and watch over you. Do not be like the horse or the mule, which have no understanding but must be controlled by bit and bridle or they will not come to you.

(Psalm 32:8-9, NIV)

Don't wait for God to yank you around like there's a bit in your mouth and guide you through rough circumstances. It is always better to simply yield to Him and listen to His still small voice.

Sometimes I have been exactly like Duke. Even though I asked God for direction, in my heart I thought I could figure things out—that I could make things happen. Consequently, I missed out on the leading of the Lord. In the New Testament the root word behind "meek" or "humble" was a word used in reference to taming wild animals including horses. Thus, when a horse was trained it was said to be "meeked" and could be used of its master.

The first step to receiving direction from God is to surrender self to Him—to yield my will to His will—to believe that He truly knows what's best. This is what humility is all about and the results will be that God can guide us.

When I develop the attitude that I don't need to rely on God's power—that I can handle life's situations by my own ingenuity, it is an evident sign that I am full of pride. If I think I can please God on the basis of my own hard work I err. A good definition of humility is that I don't put confidence in my own efforts. I like what Neil Anderson says, "Humility is confidence properly placed."[xiv]

My grandmother used to tell me the story of her conversion experience. She said that one day my grandpa came home all excited and elated over his new spiritual experience. Zealously he tried to explain to grandma how he had been "born again" and that everyone needs to have that happen. He pointed out the Scripture in John chapter three where Jesus was talking to a religious leader and said, *"I tell you the truth, unless you are born again, you cannot see the Kingdom of God"* (John 3:3). He told her that you have to give Jesus your heart and not simply give mental assent to Christian doctrine.

Grandma told me that his words made her angry. Indignantly she thought, "Who does he think he is? He's telling me I'm not good enough? Just look at my good life! I don't cuss, I don't drink. I don't run around on my husband. I'm honest. I pay my bills on time. I go to church. I believe in God. I read my Bible."

Grandma said that she stayed mad for a long time. Finally, through the persistent nudge of the Holy Spirit, she realized that she needed to humble herself and obey God's Word. She made Jesus her Lord and was wondrously "born again" and her life was forever changed. She said she almost missed heaven because she had placed her confidence in her own goodness.

When we rely on our own efforts for salvation we won't make it to heaven and when we depend on our own efforts for living a successful Christian life we are doomed to fail. There was a time in my life when I sensed that I had lost the joy of the Lord and God seemed distant. My immediate response was to try harder. I said to myself, "I will read more chapters of the Bible in my daily reading. I will pray for an hour every day. I will read more inspirational books. I will fast once a week." All of those activities are good but notice the repeated usage of the pronoun "I." It was all about my own efforts rather than a quiet confidence in Almighty God. All my hard work at getting closer to God only led to more frustration because the Spirit of God wasn't in it.

These disciplines will produce good fruit if they are coupled with a dependency on the grace and power of God. But all too often they lead to pride. Just look at the Pharisees in Jesus' day. They went to the temple to pray three times a day, fasted twice a week, tithed their income, and committed many Scriptures to memory. Yet Jesus clashed with these religionists time and time again.

A young man (I'll call him Jim) went on an extended mission trip to Mexico with a well-known evangelist. The evangelist, a powerful servant of God, insisted that his team members pray together for a minimum of one hour per day early in the morning prior to doing any ministry to the locals. When he came home he exuded a new fervor for the Lord. When I saw him some of his first words to me were, "I pray a minimum of one hour per day. How long do you pray?" Well truthfully I had not been keeping track of the length of my prayers but I did feel he was judging me and others in our congregation. Please don't get me wrong. I'm all for a vibrant prayer life. But it's all about our relationship with God, not how many hours we spend in prayer.

Paul said that if anyone had reason to boast in their own efforts he was the one. Then he proceeded to list his numerous accomplishments as a zealous Pharisee. Then he made this statement:

"I once thought these things were valuable, but now I consider them worthless because of what Christ has done. Yes, everything else is worthless when compared with the infinite value of knowing Christ Jesus my Lord. For his sake I have discarded everything else, counting it all as garbage, so that I could gain Christ and become one with him. I no longer count on my own righteousness..."
(Philippians 3:7-9a, NLB)

It is good to incorporate various disciplines in your life and to walk in integrity of character is a must. But quite subtly, that which is good can become something bad if we let pride creep in. From beginning to end our Christian walk must be characterized by a humble reliance on God's enabling ability. Our focus must be what He has done for us, not on what we have done for Him.

Three little boys were once arguing about the greatness of their fathers. The first little boy, whose father was a lawyer said, "My father is greater because he can take the guilty and make them innocent." The second boy, whose father was a doctor said, "My father is greater than that because he can make a very sick person well again!" The third little boy, whose father was a minister, was somewhat taken back by the greatness of the other fathers. Then his eyes lit up and he said, "My father is greater than either of your fathers because my father owns hell!" The other boys looked in amazement. The preacher's boy continued, "Yep, Dad came home last night after church and he said the deacons gave it to him!" That's a funny story but we as adults often do the same kind of thing, trying to prove our worth.[xv]

The truth is, we're never so small as when we're trying to be big. We all want to be great, but we don't want folks to know we want to be great. The secret of every discord in Christian homes and communities and churches is that we seek our own way and our own glory.

Someone has said, "He is a slave of the greatest slave who serves nothing but himself." Charles Kingsley wrote, "If you wish to be miserable, think much about yourself; about what you want, what you like, what respect people ought to pay you, and what people think of you."

Simon Peter, one of Jesus' original disciples, possessed an attitude of conceit and pride.

*And he (Peter) said unto him, Lord, I am ready to go with
thee, both into prison, and to death.*

(Luke 22:33, KJV)

In other words, Peter declared in a self-sufficient manner that no
matter what the devil tried to do to him he would never cease
to follow Jesus. In a parallel account in Matthew 26:33, Peter
answered and said to Him, *"Even if all are made to stumble because of You, I will never be made to stumble."* In essence he was
brashly saying that if all the other disciples fell away he would
never fall. In his conceited way of thinking he believed he was
bullet proof. The prophet Jeremiah said,

*Cursed be the man that trusteth in man and maketh flesh
his arm.*

(Jeremiah 17:5, KJV)

Someone said, "Conceit is a weird disease-it makes everybody
sick except the guy who has it." Or like the mother whale told her
baby, "When you get to the surface and start to blow, that's when
you get harpooned!" John Ruskin aptly stated, "When a man is
wrapped up in himself, he makes a pretty small package." Or, "A
big shot is frequently an individual of small caliber and immense
bore." Martin Luther wrote, "Never are men more unfit than when
they think themselves fit, and best prepared for their duty; never
more fit, then when most humbled and shamed under a sense of
their unfitness."

Stop with me at this point and say this prayer from your heart:

*Father in heaven, I ask that You make me aware of any pride
or conceit in my life (pause for a moment and listen). Please
forgive me for the times I have tried to be greater than others,
for attempting to push my way to the top to prove myself. I
repent for trusting in my own flesh rather than in Your power.*

95

*I want You to be glorified by my life. Whatever it takes, please
make me into the kind of person that You can use to strengthen
my brothers and sisters in Christ. Help me to know down deep
in my heart who I am in Christ and how much value I have to
You. I pray in the name of Your Son, Jesus Christ, Amen.*

Motives

*Though I speak with the tongues of men and of angels,
but have not love, I have become as sounding brass or
a clanging cymbal. And though I have the gift of prophecy, and understand all mysteries and all knowledge, and
though I have all faith, so that I could remove mountains,
but have not love, I am nothing. And though I bestow all
my goods to feed the poor, and though I give my body to be
burned, but have not love, it profits me nothing.*
(1 Corinthians 13:1-3, NKJV)

Why do you do the admirable things you do? Did you know you
can do religious things for the wrong reasons? Even acts of service to others can be performed out of selfish motives. Consider
the religionists of Jesus' day. When these Pharisees gave money
to the poor they made sure others around them were aware of their
generosity. They went so far as to blow trumpets announcing to
the world their acts of kindness. They did so that they might gain
the approval of the people. When they prayed they would often
stand in the synagogues and on the corners of the streets, that all
would know that they were great men of prayer. Many of them
fasted twice a week! But when they fasted they tried to look
gloomy so that everyone would be aware that they were fasting
and acknowledge that they were truly dedicated to God.

Now it is true that God teaches us to give money to those in need
and He desires for us to pray. Fasting is a powerful scriptural

discipline. But the Pharisees did these things for the wrong reasons—to exalt self.

We have another perfect example of this phenomenon in Acts 4 & 5. We see true self-giving love demonstrated as believers sold their lands and possessions to be distributed by the Apostles to meet the needs of the poor. Then Ananias and Sapphira sold a possession and pretended to give the total amount to the church (Acts 5:1-11). It was this facade, for the purpose of receiving man's praise, that brought swift judgment from God. They were merely pretending to love but in reality their motive was to look good in the eyes of the church.

Then there's the story of Simon the Sorcerer in the book of Acts. Before his conversion he astonished the people of Samaria with his magical arts. He enjoyed the fact that all the people looked up to him as someone great. When Philip preached the gospel in that region a great multitude, including Simon, responded positively and apparently placed their faith in Christ. By their hands, the apostles performed great and awesome miracles and healings. When Simon saw the remarkable demonstration of the power of the Holy Spirit through the laying on of the apostle's hands he wanted the same power. He offered them money so they would bestow upon him this same power. Now it is commendable to desire the gifts of the Spirit.

Paul says that we are to *"desire spiritual gifts"* (1 Corinthians 14:1). But clearly, Simon's attempt to gain these gifts was motivated by purely selfish reasons. Perhaps he thought that he would be able to maintain the admiration of his former audience. Peter rebuked him harshly, *"Your money perish with you, because you thought that the gift of God could be purchased with money. Repent therefore of this your wickedness..."* (Acts 8:20,22a).

Look again at the key verses above. How could I bestow all my goods to feed the poor and have not love? How could that be possible? It is clear that God is not only interested in my outward actions, though they may be commendable. More importantly, He weighs the motive of my heart. Love is not, as some suggest, simply an action. Otherwise these verses make no sense. Love requires action but action with the right motive.

Please don't be like the man who said, "I can't give tithes and of-ferings with a good attitude so I just won't give at all." No. That is a cop-out. We must obey God to generously sow into the king-dom and into the lives of other people. At the same time we need to ask God to help us give with a good attitude and pure motives.

If you honestly let the Holy Spirit search your heart you may discover that some of your Christian activities are not truly done for the glory of God. You are merely seeking your own aggran-dizement. You want to promote self. You want the praise of man because down deep inside you feel that you are of little worth.

To be transparent, I have to confess that I can remember a time when I was diligently preparing a sermon. My preparation was thorough because I wanted it to be a great message. Then the Lord spoke to me in a still small voice and said, "Why do you want it to be a good sermon?" In all honesty I had to confess that I wanted the approval of the congregation and so I repented. I changed the way I was thinking. I said, "Lord, I am going to deliver this message as unto You and for Your glory. Please speak through me what You want to say to Your people. It's not about me—it's for them and for Your glory."

Isn't that what God exhorts us to do? He says, ...*whatever you do, do all to the glory of God* (I Corinthians 10:31b). Prayerfully ask yourself, "What is my priority in life? Is it to glorify God, to extend His kingdom—or is it to glorify myself and extend my own kingdom?" You don't have to do things to prove your value.

You are already of infinite worth to the Father. Get that truth deep in your heart and you will be free to focus on God and others.

Prayer

> *Lord, forgive me for the times I have paraded my own righteousness. Forgive me for using good Christian actions to exalt myself, to prove my value. I agree with You that this sin is wicked and ungodly. I turn from this sin and by Your grace I will serve you with a pure heart, In Jesus' name, Amen.*

False Humility

> *And be renewed in the spirit of your mind; and that ye put on the new man, which after God is created in **true** righteousness and **true** holiness.*
> (Ephesians 4:23-24, KJV, emphasis mine)

People with the valueless spirit often appear to be quite humble. I ministered to a man that everyone thought was very humble. One time at work his employer introduced him to a group of employees as "the humblest man he knew." Through ministry, however, we discovered his humility was really false-humility. I told him that true humility is the ability to see yourself as you truly are, not less than you are.

True humility does not necessitate self-deprecation. That is false humility. In the book of Numbers we read that . . .*Moses was the most humble person in all the world.* (Num. 12:3, CEV). Now that is a pretty amazing statement to say about anyone but it especially startled me one day when someone pointed out that Moses wrote the book of Numbers and, therefore, made this claim about himself! Thus, it is okay to speak well of your own strengths in the right situation and setting and it is not wrong to allow others to assess your abilities in a positive light.

I heard a story about a church that was teaching on humility. They decided they would honor the most humble person in the congregation so they voted in order to determine who would receive the humble button award. The church almost unanimously selected a certain man and called him up in front to receive the humble button. But when he went forward to receive his award they took it away from him for being willing to receive it! That's a funny story but somehow we also have it in our minds that it is wrong to receive an accurate appraisal of our good character traits. This mistaken notion represents false humility.

I remember complimenting a pastor one Sunday about his good sermon. He responded, "Oh, that wasn't me, it was God." His reaction seems praiseworthy on the surface. However, not only did he discount my attempt to encourage him but he demonstrated false humility. False humility manifests itself by refusing to accept praise and compliments. When someone compliments you it is best to simply respond by saying thank you.

Now, at the same time, as you acknowledge the compliment, in your heart you must deflect the praise to God. Always say a silent prayer, "Thank you God for giving me the grace to do what I did." True humility is recognizing I am where I am today because of God and other people.[xvi] False humility makes it hard to respond in the right way to a compliment.

Another way false humility comes out is through self-abasement, by constantly feeling others are smarter or better looking than you. Many people were shocked by the results of a survey taken several years ago of twelve well-known actors. They were asked to list the changes they would make in their facial appearance. Most of them listed between four and twelve alterations they would make in their personal appearance. None of them was completely satisfied.[xvii]

Just as there exists a false humility there also remains a counter-feit selflessness. Remember, pride and selfishness are two sides of the same coin and are related. In the same way, false pride and false selflessness are also linked. It is not only necessary to die to pride; we also must die to the self-focused life. To keep us from getting out of balance it is important to point out what death to self does not mean, otherwise, the devil can twist this teaching to his advantage.

First, it does not mean that we lose our identity or individuality—that is Eastern philosophy. The Bible indicates that even in the afterlife there is a continuity between who we are now and who we will be then. For example, the disciples recognized, perhaps by listening to the conversation, that Moses and Elijah were present on the Mount of Transfiguration. Moses and Elijah did not lose their identity after they died and went to heaven—they continued to uniquely be who they were on earth. In the afterlife we will recognize our loved ones and others who have died in Christ.

Individuality is seen in another way in the natural realm. God created each one of us in His image and yet we are all unique. No two people have identical DNA, finger prints, voice prints, or irises. Even identical twins who share the same genetic makeup have different fingerprints. God designed us to be unique. Rather than losing our individuality we must celebrate it. The Bible says, *I praise you because of the wonderful way you created me* (Psalm 139:14a, CEV).

Second, it does not mean that we are to give up any sense of pleasure. God Himself takes pleasure in many things and created us to enjoy beauty as well. Otherwise, why did He create the numerous varieties of flowers and trees? Why did He create the various species of beautifully colored fish and birds? Read the Song of

Solomon and discover that God intends for a man and wife to take pleasure in each other.

Third, it does not necessarily mean that we have to lose interest in amusements such as hobbies, sports, or music. It is just that we don't want anything other than God to take first place. Dying to self is not necessarily a matter of moving into a monastery and meditating on God all day. He expects us to be equipped to engage our culture in meaningful dialogue as 21st-century people.

Fourth, it does not imply that we are to hate ourselves or inflict self-punishment. In the Philippines there lives a group of people known as Black Catholics. Every Good Friday these religionists practice flogging themselves and crawling on broken glass in order to do penance. Some of them even volunteer to be hung on a cross with nails driven through their hands and feet. Unfortunately, though they seem devout, they do not consider the true extent of Jesus' finished work on the cross. God has already taken our punishment for our sins upon Himself.

Fifth, it does not mean that we have no boundaries, that to say no is always an act of selfishness. If I said yes to every request for my energy and time there would be nothing of me left to give to those things God has set as priorities in life. There are a lot of good causes that vie for my attention, but God does not want me to settle for the good when I can have the best. Learning to say no can be a good thing.

I hope you can see that it is easy to get in a ditch when it comes to humility and selflessness. Therefore, we must ask God to help us avoid this tendency and to deliver us from false humility and false selflessness.

I heard about a lady who owned 65 charm schools across the United States. She made a tidy sum in royalties on each one of those schools. She had a radio program with a listening audience of 10 million people. But she became dissatisfied with her life and didn't know what was wrong. Through reading *Pilgrim's Progress* she gave her life to Christ. When she read the passage of Scripture about dying to self (Luke 9:23-24) she thought that meant she had to reduce her life to complete physical barrenness. So she disengaged from the charm schools and moved out of her beautiful home. Then she moved into a trailer with her two children. She let her physical appearance deteriorate to where she looked like a homeless bag lady.

Tragically she took this important teaching of Jesus and twisted it. Is this what Jesus requires? No, He actually demands something much deeper than giving up money and beauty. He asks that we surrender our hearts to Him—to give up a self-directed life.

Finally, a man of God confronted the woman with the truth that she had gotten into a theological ditch. Her eyes were opened and she exclaimed, "Oh, I see what I've been doing. I've been reducing my life to that of a vegetable and calling it victory." After seeing the error of her ways she got her life in godly balance. There are those who say that when you truly give your life to Jesus that you give up all worldly pleasures. Jesus demands something much greater—that you surrender yourself. That's the one thing you own. Then when you give yourself to Him He gives you back your life with brand new meaning. In this way you lose your life in order to really find it. Jesus said, *I have come that they might have life, and that they might have it more abundantly* (John 10:10b, KJV).

Prayer

Father in heaven, I turn away from all false humility. I ask that You bring those structures to death at the cross. Help me to live in true humility. I ask that You help me die to self according to Your will for my life. Keep me from false humility and from false selflessness, in Jesus Name, Amen.

10

Envy/jealousy, Anger, Rebellion

Envy/jealousy often flows from the valueless spirit—from not knowing who you really are in Christ. If you don't deal with envy/jealousy you won't be able to rid yourself of the valueless spirit. Envy/jealousy is a strong and insidious subsidiary spirit which serves as armor to the valueless strongman helping to lock it in. Even though it wreaks severe havoc in our lives, the tragic truth is that few people recognize when they walk in the spirit of envy/jealousy.

After over 30 years of ministry I finally had one person come to me for pastoral counseling asking for help with envy/jealousy. I congratulated her that she was the first to seek my help in overcoming this stronghold. I suppose it is rare for us to acknowledge this sin, in part, due to the fact that we are ashamed to admit when it's operating in us.

This sin of the flesh seems so petty and childish when brought out into the open that we tend to play it down or try to ignore it. But God thinks it is so important to deal with that He made one of His Ten Commandments address the subject. *"Thou shalt not covet."*

Keep in mind that covetousness is a form of envy/jealousy.

Envy/jealousy opens a person up to a host of tormenting problems. First, envy/jealousy leads to strife. Scripture repeatedly ties envy and strife together.

> *Let us walk properly as in the day, not in revelry and drunkenness, not in lewdness and lust, not in <u>strife</u> and <u>envy.</u>*
>
> (Romans 13:13, NKJV, emphases mine)

> *For you are still carnal. For where there are <u>envy, strife,</u> and divisions among you, are you not carnal and behaving like mere men?*
>
> (1 Corinthians 3:3, NKJV)

> *He is proud, knowing nothing, but is obsessed with disputes and arguments over words, from which come <u>envy, strife</u>, reviling, evil suspicions.*
>
> (1 Timothy 6:4, NKJV)

Envy and strife go together. Therefore, if there is strife in your life, look for envy.

Second, some health problems can be traced to the spiritual root of envy/jealousy.

> *A sound heart is life to the body, but envy is rottenness to the bones.*
>
> (Proverbs 14:30, NKJV)

The immune system has its origin in the bone marrow and envy/jealousy will weaken your body's ability to fight off disease. Scripture teaches that you will live longer if you avoid covetousness (a form of envy/jealousy).

But he who hates covetousness will prolong his days.
(Proverbs 28:16b, NKJV)

Covetousness is actually a form of envy/jealousy and covetousness will cause you to miss out on your spiritual inheritance.

For this you know, that no fornicator, unclean person, nor covetous man, who is an idolater, has any inheritance in the kingdom of Christ and God.
(Ephesians 5:5, NKJV)

God has great blessings in store for His children but envy/jealousy will keep us from receiving.

In addition, envy may bring confusion.

But if you have bitter envy and self-seeking in your hearts, do not boast and lie against the truth. This wisdom does not descend from above, but is earthly, sensual, demonic. For where envy and self-seeking exist, confusion and every evil thing will be there.
(James 3:14-16, NKJV)

Do you have confusion in your life? Look for envy.

Another problem with envy/jealousy is that it produces bitterness. When Joseph's brothers experienced the preferential treatment meted out by their father, their hearts brimmed with envy. "*And his brothers envied him*" (Genesis 37:11a). Sadly, their envy turned to bitterness and they conspired to kill Joseph. Later the oldest brother convinced them not to commit murder so instead they ended up selling him into slavery. Then they lied to their father implying that a wild animal killed Joseph. The writer of Hebrews warns us of the consequences of bitterness.

Looking diligently lest anyone fall short of the grace of God; lest any root of bitterness springing up cause trouble, and by this many become defiled. . .

(Hebrews 12:15, NKJV)

Since so much is at stake, it behooves us to investigate the dynamics of this sin. As I previously stated, it sometimes enters our life through the valueless spirit. But envy and jealousy also come in through the fear of loss. In Hebrew 13:5-6 we read, *Let your conversation (life style) be without <u>covetousness</u> and be content with such things as ye have. For he hath said, 'I will never leave thee nor forsake thee,' so that we may boldly say the Lord is my helper, I will not <u>fear</u> what man shall do unto me* (KJV). Do you see the connection God places between envy/jealousy and fear?

When Saul heard the women singing *"Saul has slain his thousands and David his ten thousands,"* Saul was obviously envious and jealous. But the scripture says, in that context, that he was afraid of David. Interestingly, the Lord refers to fear in that context at least four different times. Why? The answer is because envy/jealousy often originates with fear, or fear of loss to be more specific.

The religious leaders delivered Jesus to Pontius Pilate out of envy (Matthew 27:18). They feared that His growing popularity would cause them to lose their influence over the masses. Again we see an example that the fear of loss leads to envy.

Because of our society's twisted values, women often struggle with envy/jealousy when they see another woman whom they perceive to be prettier, better dressed, and shapelier. The emotion behind the envy/jealousy is fear—fear that they will go unnoticed—fear that they will not be appreciated, recognized—fear that they will lose their value. This fear then leads to self-bitterness.

How do you know if envy/jealousy is operating in your life? Sharon, a struggling single mom, belonged to a cell group sponsored by her church that met weekly in homes. At each meeting they shared a meal, sang Christian songs, studied the Bible, and prayed for each other's needs. The custom involved a rotation whereby they took turns holding the gatherings in a different member's home every week. Sharon loved the support and fellowship her small group provided, but she also enjoyed the aspect of seeing the inside of the beautiful homes in the upscale community where the church was located.

Sharon was always the first one to compliment the host on their lovely home. "Oh, you have a beautiful home," she often remarked enthusiastically. "God has really blessed you!" But inwardly, Sharon was thinking, "This is very nice, but what about me?" What was Sharon wrestling with? A spirit of envy/jealousy. And what was this demon doing? It was robbing her of her joy. Rather than being content and grateful for what she had, fear began to get a hold in her heart that God was withholding something good—fear that she had lost God's favor.

Ivor was a decent musician. Although his skills were limited he played the piano well enough and possessed an above average voice. The mission church he attended quickly enlisted him to lead the worship team on Sunday mornings. The music program went well during the fledgling first couple of years as the church became established. As the church grew, gradually other more capable musicians volunteered their services.

One day a new recruit was asked to play the keyboard and sing a solo during Sunday morning worship. It was immediately obvious to all that he was a highly gifted musician with a special anointing for bringing the congregation into the presence of God. Before the pastor started his sermon that morning he heaped lavish praise upon the special music. Then after the service while people fellowshipped in the foyer, one by one members approached Ivor mentioning how much they enjoyed the special music and wished the individual would perform again soon.

Ivor smiled agreeing with their assessment but inwardly discomfort gnawed at his insides. Thoughts raced through his mind, "I work hard volunteering my services week after week and where is the thanks I get?" Ivor was battling envy, a common phenomenon amongst musicians. If it bothers you when other people receive the praise for doing the same things you do, then you are struggling with a spirit of envy/jealousy. If you feel threatened when someone comes along who is more highly gifted than you in the area of your expertise, than envy/jealousy more than likely presents a problem for you.

Another way to discern envy is to ask yourself if you often make comparisons. Do you tend to compare your income, talents, education, or accomplishments with that of others? The apostle Paul had this to say about comparisons:

For we dare not class ourselves or compare ourselves with those who commend themselves. But they, measuring themselves by themselves, and comparing themselves among themselves, are not wise.
(2 Corinthians 10:12, NKJV)

It is foolish to seek self worth by making comparisons because there will always be people better looking, more intelligent, wealthier, more talented, and successful. Our self worth comes from God's estimation. He promised to never leave us or forsake us. Therefore we must have great value to Him just the way we are.

I encourage you to take a spiritual inventory. If you often experience confusion and strife in your life the root cause may be envy/jealousy. If there is a problem with your immune system the spiritual basis may be envy/jealousy. If you struggle with lack of contentment and joy or unresolved anger, the root may be traced back to envy/jealousy. If you tend to compare yourself to others, look for envy/jealousy. It would be wise for you to ask God to reveal any envy/jealousy that might be lurking in the recesses of your heart. Recognition is 90% of the victory when dealing with any stronghold. But envy is so subtle it takes the illuminating power of the Holy Spirit to enable us to see it.

Don't go into morbid introspection or conjure up something that is not really there. But if God reveals that you are disposed to harbor envy/jealousy in your life I encourage you to pray the following prayer.

Prayer

Heavenly Father, I agree with You that envy/jealousy/covetousness is sin and I repent. This sin is wicked, ungodly, and against You. Because of this sin I rightfully deserve death on a cross. But I thank You Lord Jesus that You died in my place. I receive Your forgiveness. The blood of Jesus cleanses me now and I am free, I am forgiven. Lord, I ask You to bring the structure of this fleshly tendency to death at the cross of Christ. And now envy/jealousy/covetousness, I reject you, I renounce you, and I break any agreement I ever made with you. I command you to leave me now and go to dry places, in the name of Jesus Christ, Amen.[xiii]

Anger

Most people with the valueless spirit are angry at God. They believe that since God made them, and they have no value, then

God is to be blamed for all of their problems. The vast majority of the people I have ministered to have had a very difficult time admitting to their anger. Perhaps subconsciously they reason that anger directed toward God will incur His wrath and they fear His judgment.

Behind the anger lies the belief that they could do a better job at being God, though they would never say that in so many words. Many people have judged God because they don't agree with the way He did things or at least allowed them to happen.

If you are indeed angry at God He already knows all about it. He knows the depth of your anger and doesn't love you any less for it. But you need to let it out by telling God how you feel. If your anger stays bottled up inside you it will poison your soul and ruin your intimate walk with the Lord. Read the Psalms and see how David dealt honestly with his emotions. He poured out his complaint to the Lord.

> *With my voice I cry out to the LORD; with my voice I plead for mercy to the LORD. I pour out my complaint before him; I tell my trouble before him.*
> (Psalm 142:1-2, ESV, emphasis mine)

If you have anger in your heart toward God, pray this prayer with me now:

> *Father in heaven, I recognize that I am angry at You. I forgive you from my heart for all the things I perceived that You did and did not do for me. (Tell God what you perceived He did or did not do for you. Say it out loud. Pour out your complaint to Him. Don't sugar-coat it.) I let you go free. I lay nothing to your charge. I forgive you from my heart simply because You have already forgiven me. Now I release blessings to You. Please make me a blessing to You.*[xix] *I repent*

*for having judged You God. My judgment against You was
sin. I forgive myself for my judgments and anger against You.
I receive your forgiveness and I let myself go free, in Jesus'
Name, Amen.*

Rebellion

Saul approached the prophet Samuel hoping to gain supernatural
direction to find his father's lost donkeys. Samuel told him,

> *"As for your donkeys that were lost three days ago, do not
> set your mind on them, for they have been found. And for
> whom is all that is desirable in Israel? Is it not for you and
> for all your father's house?" Saul answered, "Am I not a
> Benjaminite, from the least of the tribes of Israel? And
> is not my clan the humblest of all the clans of the tribe of
> Benjamin? Why then have you spoken to me in this way?"*
> (1 Samuel 9:20-21, ESV)

Saul's response sounds commendable at first glance but do his
words demonstrate true humility? No! Scripture also says that
Saul was "little in his own eyes."

> *And Samuel said, "Though you are little in your own eyes,
> are you not the head of the tribes of Israel? The LORD
> anointed you king over Israel."*
> (1 Samuel 15:17, ESV)

However, this represents false humility. True humility is "the
willingness to be known for who we really are and to take God's
side against sin."[xx] True humility is a matter of seeing ourselves
as we really are. True humility sees no need to denigrate ourselves. Saul's false humility stemmed from the valueless spirit
and the valueless spirit provided fertile soil for other sins to grow,

especially rebellion. Almost immediately after Samuel told King Saul he was "little in his own eyes" he made this defining statement regarding Saul's life:

> *And Samuel Said, "Has the LORD as great delight in burnt offerings and sacrifices, as in obeying the voice of the LORD? Behold, to obey is better than sacrifice, and to listen than the fat of rams. ²³For rebellion is as the sin of divination, and presumption is as iniquity and idolatry. Because you have rejected the word of the LORD, he has also rejected you from being king."*
>
> (1 Samuel 15:22-23, ESV)

God makes a connection between rebellion and the valueless spirit.

Not all rebellion has its basis in the valueless spirit but it often does. Valueless sufferers tend to think they know better than God and insist on doing things their own way just like Saul. Remember, I said previously that they have a hard time trusting God. They don't like who they are and they blame God for making them that way. Saul thought his plan was superior to God's.

Rebellion opens the door to the demonic in a person's life. The Bible teaches that rebellion is in the same category of sin as divination (witchcraft), a highly demonic practice. Rebellion will cut you off from God and you will find yourself in a dry land spiritually.

> *God settles the solitary in a home; he leads out the prisoners to prosperity, but the rebellious dwell in a parched land.*
>
> (Psalm 68:6, ESV)

Prayer

Lord, if I have rebellion in my life, please show me. Shine your light in my heart so that nothing can remain hidden. Help me to see me the way You see me so that I might come to hate rebellious tendencies in my life. I bring this tendency to death at the cross of Christ. I reject and renounce rebellion and break any agreement with this sin, in Jesus' name, Amen.

11

Drivenness, Performance, etc.

Drivenness

Paul Tournier, the famous Christian physician and counselor, has written some interesting comments regarding childhood trauma. He observed that a large number of the world's prominent leaders had one thing in common: they shared the unpleasant experience of having been orphans. Many of these super achievers suffered the pain of childhood abuse and severe mistreatment. "This is confirmed in numerous studies of high performers," writes Tournier. "As many as three-fourths of those who become celebrated achievers are estimated to have suffered serious emotional deprivation or hardship in childhood. Because they feel so worthless inside, they will work themselves practically to death trying to have some value. And, as a result of that, many of them become successful."[xxi]

Many of our nation's top executives suffer from drivenness. Merriam-Webster defines drivenness as, "having a compulsive or urgent quality, a driven sense of obligation." Drivenness is behind workaholism, the most socially acceptable addiction. Workaholics tend to keep excessively long hours at work, talk much about their achievements, have a hard time saying no, and have difficulty resting or relaxing. Drivenness usually arises from a sense of valuelessness deep within the human spirit. Value is linked to what they do rather than who they are. Driven people fail to accept, and rest in, the unconditional love of God. Such people tend to focus their energies on activities that bolster their sense of value, and this activity becomes an addiction.

Wayne Oates, pastor and psychologist, jokingly compared himself to an alcoholic. He said he started with "social" working, boasting about how much work he could "hold" and how he could work others "under the table." This behavior progressed to a true addiction and before he knew it he was hooked. Dr. Oates said he would "pass out," (become emotionally dead) usually after he got home from the office. Well-meaning friends advised him to slow down but when he did he suffered "withdrawal symptoms."[xxii] Workaholics dread family vacations and holidays unless they can combine the time off with work.

According to Barbara Killinger, workaholics gradually become "emotionally crippled and addicted to control and power in a compulsive drive to gain approval and success."[xiii] Many godly men and women, even well-respected pastors are workaholics.

Though they often achieve great "success," there is an awful price to be paid. Their marriage and family usually suffer the greatest. A pastor's wife told her over-worked husband one day, "If the church was a woman I'd snatch her bald-headed!" Now that's a woman that felt neglected. The children of workaholics also feel abandoned because mom or dad doesn't have enough time or energy left for them. The Bible sums up the workaholic condition with these words,

For all his days are sorrowful, and his work burdensome;

even in the night his heart takes no rest. This also is vanity.

(Ecclesiastes 2:23, NKJV)

Performance Orientation

Workaholism develops in the heart of a child when love is conditional and based on performance. The child gets praise only as a result of their accomplishments and the parents fail to communicate acceptance for who the child is. The lie, "my value is in what I do," gets inculcated at an early age. The child concludes, for example, that if I make my bed and clean my room perfectly then mommy will love me. Children reared in such home environments often grow up to be overly involved in work—working to earn an income, working around the house, volunteering in non-profit organizations, etc. They work hard, usually to avoid the emotional pain of the valueless spirit.

Barbara Killinger says, "Conditional love teaches a child to be dependent on others for approval; unconditional love encourages independent appraisal, objectivity, and self-affirmation in deserved pride."[xxiv] As an adult the individual believes that he has to perform to be accepted. If you suffer from performance orientation I recommend you turn to the appendix at the back of this book and pray now the prayer that was developed by Elijah House Ministries.

The Poverty Spirit

The flip side of drivenness is what the Bible calls sloth. *The desire of the slothful kills him, for his hands refuse to labor* (Proverbs 21:25, AMP). Scripture clearly teaches that God wants us to have a good work ethic.

Let him that stole steal no more: but rather let him labour, working with his hands the thing which is good, that he may have to give to him that needeth.

(Ephesians 4:28, KJV)

You lazy people can learn by watching an anthill. Ants don't have leaders, but they store up food during harvest season. How long will you lie there doing nothing at all? When are you going to get up and stop sleeping? Sleep a little. Doze a little. Fold your hands and twiddle your thumbs. Suddenly, everything is gone, as though it had been taken by an armed robber.

(Proverbs 6:6-11, CEV)

While drivenness can have bad consequences, the other side of the ditch is laziness. Laziness, however, often arises out of fear, not just a stubborn refusal to work. Scripture bears this out in Proverbs 22:13, KJV, *The slothful man saith, There is a lion without, I shall be slain in the streets.* This verse teaches that a slothful or lazy man won't go out and do his work because he is afraid that a lion will attack him out on the road. What is the "lion" they fear? They fear the pain involved in becoming successful. They fear the discomfort of doing what it takes to get ahead and they don't want to pay the price. They avoid the pain of the daily discipline required to reach their goals and accomplish their dreams.

The Spirit of Poverty

This spirit of poverty is much different than the poverty spirit. Whereas the poverty spirit is connected to the avoidance of the pain involved in success, the spirit of poverty is coupled with the valueless spirit. The spirit of poverty tells the individual that they are not worthy of success, that they deserve to struggle financially. Because they doubt their intrinsic value they have a hard time receiving. When you take two magnets and try to connect them, positive to positive pole or negative to negative pole, it doesn't work. There's an invisible magnetic force that repels the magnets from each other. Similarly, the spirit of poverty pushes away money or other provisions even though you work hard, tithe, claim God's promises, pray, and do the other things necessary to succeed. It's almost uncanny how money seems to be driven away.

Perfectionism

Charles' mother gave him the task of pulling all the dandelions out of the lawn in the front yard. She gave him a special tool made for that purpose and a box of 33 gallon plastic trash bags for disposing of the weeds. Then she instructed her 11-year old son to finish the job by the time she returned from shopping. Charles worked hard in the hot sun to pull the hundreds of weeds up by the roots so they wouldn't grow back. He wanted to do a good job for his mom. Four hours later several of his bags were full and mom came home pulling the car up in the driveway. Beaming with pride he approached his mother, "I'm done. Look at all the weeds I got up," lifting the bag for her to see. Scanning the lawn her eyes fell on one tiny weed he'd overlooked and she pointed at it and said, "You forgot that one."

How do you think Charles felt? Of course he felt deflated. But he received a lie that affected him the rest of his life. He believed the lie that says, "I can't get anything right no matter how hard I try." Charles mother was a classic perfectionist. Perfectionists often discourage their children because their unreasonable expectations make them want to give up. If you had a perfectionist parent you probably received the valueless spirit.

His mother did the same thing regarding his grades at school. He showed his mother his report card one day. He had earned

A's, B's and one C. His mother looked at that C and said, next time you better not have any C's. Consequently, he worked a lot harder on his studies and next time his report card showed all A's except for one A minus. The teacher added a comment saying, "Charles has shown much improvement." When his mother saw that A minus she said harshly, "Next time have all A's." Her perfectionism continued to water the seed of the valueless lie, "No matter how hard I try I'll never get it right. Something must be wrong with me."

In the above scenario guys like Charles will often receive the lie that says, "I have more value if I do things perfectly." This causes them to seek their worth out of doing their work perfectly, even to the point of being obsessive. If Charles doesn't deal with his perfectionism he will do the same thing to his children that his mother did to him.

Quest for Significance

Tony approached his pastor with a concern he had about the cleanliness of the church buildings. Their small Baptist church employed a janitorial service that sometimes didn't do a thorough job of cleaning and some of the people were complaining. He said, "Pastor, I believe God has given me the spiritual gift of service and I would like to bless the church by offering my services to clean our buildings every week. I used to own my own janitorial business so I know how to get everything in tip top shape. I don't believe God has called me to teach or preach or do anything in the public eye. I'm content to serve our Lord quietly in the background and if I had this job in the church I would feel like I'm doing my part.

The pastor met with his deacons and they gladly gave Tony the job and paid him what they had been paying the previous janitorial service even though he didn't ask for money. Tony did superb work keeping the place clean, happily serving as the janitor and many people commented on how great the buildings looked. However, after six weeks Tony once again requested a meeting with the pastor. He said, "Pastor, I've been thinking and praying a lot about what I'm supposed to do in our church and I really believe God has given me the gift of teaching. I've been doing a great deal of study related to the Jewish Feasts in the Old Testament and I would like to teach an eight-week class in the adult Sunday School class." The church was in need of a teacher for that class and after some discussion the pastor agreed, though somewhat reluctantly.

The class actually went well, to the pastor's delight, and some people reported to him how much they were learning. Tony spent hours and hours every week studying for his class. One Sunday the pastor met Tony after church and congratulated him on a job well-done. At that point Tony said to the pastor, "You know Pastor, I've been thinking. I don't have the time to do both the cleaning job and prepare to teach this class. I'm going to need to give up the cleaning job. I believe God has given me the spiritual gift of teaching and I will have a much greater impact on the kingdom of God if I use my talents in this way." So the church had to find another janitorial service.

This pattern of searching for a meaningful position continued. For instance, after the eight-week series on the Old Testament Feasts, Tony wanted to try his hand as a musician in the worship band. Then after a short stint as the bass guitarist on the worship team Tony dropped out of the band and asked to be on the deacon board. By this time, however, the dysfunction in Tony became apparent to the church leadership and they graciously declined to accept him as a candidate for the office of deacon. Shortly after that Tony approached the pastor with the news that he desired to become involved in the Anglican Church because he loved the beauty of their liturgy and their strong sense of church history.

After Tony left the Baptist church the pastor lost contact with him for about eight years. Then one day they happened to run into each other at a nearby restaurant and the pastor asked Tony if he was still an Anglican and how that was going for him. Tony said, "Well pastor, I was eventually ordained a deacon in the Anglican Church and I did that for about a year. Now I'm taking a hiatus and I'm looking around, attending different churches. I haven't been to the Anglican Church for over a year now. I might join a Messianic church that I like here in the area."

What is behind Tony's wanderlust? Why does he have difficulty sticking to a job given him? In his particular case he is on a quest for a sense of significance. He wants his life to count for something that will help him overcome his lack of value. But no matter what he does in the church he will never find value in what he does. He is running on the wrong track and serving God with the wrong motives. As long as he doesn't deal with the valueless spirit in his life he will never be satisfied or feel fulfilled by what he does.

On this note I will address a problem I see running rampant in the Body of Christ. Sometimes it appears to me that every committed Christian wants to be in a paid full-time ministry. They are tired of their secular job and they want to do ministry. They feel like they aren't making a difference with their lives serving the corporate world and they want to impact others with the life-changing message of the Gospel of Christ. On the one hand, this desire is commendable because the Lord has commanded each one of us to let our light shine and be witnesses for Him. On the other hand, this tendency is often tied to the valueless spirit as these individuals are on a holy quest to find significance in their lives. For them ministry has become an idol.

Every born-again Christian needs to know that they already have a ministry. Their primary ministry is to the Lord Himself. Just to serve Jesus—to worship Him, to bless Him, and to obey Him is my primary calling. Let me ask you this: If you never have a "ministry," if you never get to teach or preach or lead music, is Jesus enough? Are you content just knowing Him and ministering to Him? If not, you have made ministry an idol and you need to repent. Your first and foremost goal should be to minister to Jesus.

Only those who truly know who they are in Christ are free enough to make serving Jesus their primary goal of ministry. My performance oriented friends read the story of Mary and Martha and identify with Martha. They come to her defense claiming that she gets a bad rap and ignore the fact that in this gospel story Martha gets a gentle rebuke from our Lord. Read that story again;

> *Now as they went on their way, Jesus entered a village. And a woman named Martha welcomed him into her house. And she had a sister called Mary, who sat at the Lord's feet and listened to his teaching. But Martha was distracted with much serving. And she went up to him and said, "Lord, do you not care that my sister has left me to serve alone? Tell her then to help me." But the Lord answered her, "Martha, Martha, you are anxious and troubled about many things, but one thing is necessary. Mary has chosen the good portion, which will not be taken away from her."*
>
> (Luke 10:38-42, ESV)

Beloved, you are already of great significance regardless of what you do vocationally. Years ago I attended a pastors' conference in Southern California led by Peter Lord and Jack Taylor. I'll never forget Peter Lord's question. He asked us pastors, "Who has more worth, you or Jesus?" Somewhat taken back by the seeming stupidity of the question, most of us answered, "Jesus, of course."

But he challenged us to rethink our answer. If Jesus lives in us and we live in Him, if we are literally a part of His body, if we, as it says in Romans, are *"joint-heirs with Christ,"* then we are of equal value with Christ in the mind of Father God. My value is not in what I do but in who I am. I am a child of the King and I'm in Jesus and He's in me.

How do we determine the value of an object? I went to a car show with my family recently. At this show they had a vintage Ferrari with a price tag of nearly a million dollars! I was surprised by that amount, but is the car really worth that much? It is only if someone is willing to pay that much. You can put your house on the market for $500,000 but is it worth that much if people are only willing to give you $200,000 for it? No. True value is determined by the price someone is willing to pay.

How much was God willing to pay for you? He paid the inestimable price of His own dear Son. When God offered up His Son Jesus to die on the cross in our place He proved once and for all how much we are worth to Him. I don't do ministry to receive value, I do ministry out of gratitude for His incalculable love for me.

The Religious Spirit

I definitely don't want to promote religion through this book. My desire is to lift up Jesus. Religion will get you in trouble every time. The religionists were the ones that gave Jesus most of His trouble. It is amazing to me that even though phariseeism was the biggest problem Jesus had to face during His ministry on earth, we have very few books exposing the problem today. It seems strange to me that you can find dozens of books on every ism and schism known to man but you are hard pressed to find a book on the number one problem that Jesus faced. Could it be that we have a blind spot? The truth be known, there is probably a little bit of phariseeism in every one of us. Most people just don't see it. (I use the terms "phariseeism" and "religious spirit" almost synonymously.)

Jesus had little trouble with demons during His earthly ministry. They were cast out just by His word. It was the conservative, zealous religious establishment that represented His greatest foe. Those who were the most zealous for the word of God crucified the Word Himself when he became man and walked among us. The same is true today. All the cults and false religions combined have not done as much damage to the true moves of God as the opposition, or infiltration, of the religious spirit. Cults and false religions are easily discerned, but the religious spirit has thwarted or diverted possibly every revival or move of the Spirit through-out history.

One major problem the Pharisees had was that they struggled with grace. A great English preacher at the turn of the century said, "If you have preached on grace and have not yet been accused of lasciviousness, you have not yet preached on grace." Grace is in such conflict with religion that there is always a battle between the two. Religion says, "Do." Grace says, "Believe what Jesus will do and has already done." Religion says, "Strive." Grace says, "Cease striving and enter Christ's rest." Preachers of re-ligion focus on you and the rules. Preachers of grace focus on Christ and the flow of His life within you. Preachers of religion preach from Mount Sinai (law). Preachers of grace preach from Mount Calvary (grace). Preachers of religion bring guilt and con-demnation into the lives of their hearers. Preachers of grace bring freedom and release and peace into the hearts of their hearers.

Lent, in Christian tradition, is the period of the liturgical year leading up to Easter. The traditional purpose of Lent is the prepa-ration of the believer — through prayer, penitence, almsgiving and self-denial. Many believers practice the Biblical discipline of fasting at this time of year. Giving up certain things at this season can be a good thing if done in the right spirit. In the first century Palestine there were three major expressions of Orthodox Judaism: alms giving, certain prescribed prayers, and twice weekly fasting, on Mondays and Thursdays. This fasting schedule was kept in commemoration of Moses going up to Mt. Sinai on the fifth day and coming down from the mountain on the second day of the week. Clearly to the Pharisees, a powerful religious sect in Jesus' day, the concept of fasting was extremely important and I agree with them.

The Pharisees took these practices very seriously and carefully followed them faithfully. The problem is not with these disciplines but with their public display and ostentatious show. When they gave money for the poor, they blew trumpets so everyone could see how spiritual they were. (See Matt. 6:2). When they prayed they did it in such a way as to be seen by men. (See Matt. 6:5). When they fasted they actually whitened their faces, put ashes on their heads, wore their clothes in shoddy disarray, refused to wash and looked as gloomy as possible so that everyone would know they were fasting. (See Matt. 6:16). Their religion was not a matter of humility, repentance, or forgiveness, but of ceremony and proud display. So that their external rituals, that were supposed to be signs of righteousness, were actually displays of godlessness.

Sadly, most people who have a spirit of religion have not the foggiest idea that they have it. Like the Pharisees, they think they are truly serving God. Religious ritual and routine have always been dangers to true godliness. If we are not careful, good things we do, such as going to church, reading the Bible, saying grace before meals, singing praise choruses and fasting, can become lifeless routines without any Holy Spirit inspired joy.

Erma Bombeck tells how she was sitting in church one Sunday when a small child turned around and began to smile at the people behind her. She was just smiling, not making a sound. When the mother noticed, she said in a staged whisper, "Stop that grinning—you're in church," gave her a swat, and said, "That's better!" Erma concluded that some people come to church looking like they had just read the will of their rich aunt and learned that she had given everything to her pet hamster!

I read about a man who used to teach that Christians should never smile or laugh because never once does the Bible say Jesus ever laughed or smiled. Arguments from silence will get you in trouble. Doesn't the Bible say in Hebrews 1:9 that Jesus was anointed with the oil of joy?

The truth is that phariseeism, or the religious spirit, does not represent Christianity at all. Consider the fact that Jesus connected phariseeism with the spirit of murder (John 8:44). Even Paul, a committed Pharisee, sought to destroy churches and murder Christians before he was gloriously converted on the road to Damascus. In my opinion the religious spirit endangers Christians more than any other error, even more than the New Age Movement. I know it has hindered my personal walk with God more than anything else.

In John 8:44 Jesus harshly asserted that the Pharisees were of the devil—that is, they were demonically inspired and there was no truth in them. Jesus is saying to you today that if you operate out of a religious spirit you don't really know God. Because modern-day Pharisees are not open to the voice of the Holy Spirit they miss out on the moves of God in their generation. For example, notice that no Pharisees were present at the birth of Jesus even though it represented the most significant act in human history. In contrast, the Magi, who studied the stars, were wise enough to discern that they needed to show up to worship the Christ-Child.

A lot can be written about the religious spirit or phariseeism but it is beyond the scope of this book to deal with this problem thoroughly. In this writing I want to focus on the religious spirit as it relates to the valueless spirit. Here are some tenants of phariseeism that flow from the valueless spirit.

First, the religious spirit would have us depend on human strength and wisdom in place of the power of God. The Sadducees, another religious sect of Jesus' day, did not believe in the supernatural. Paul said, *For the kingdom of God is not in word but in power* (1 Corinthians 4:20, NKJV). The valueless spirit makes us want to depend on our own strength. If I believe that I am of no intrinsic value and I believe that God created me, then I will also believe that I can't trust God, that I will have to rely on my own ability.

Second, it is founded upon zeal for God. Paul wrote of his Jewish brethren in Romans 10:2, *For I bear them witness that they have a zeal for God, but not according to knowledge* (ESV). This is the deceptive nature of the religious spirit. No one on earth prayed more, fasted more, read the Bible more, had a greater hope in the coming of the Messiah, or had more zeal for the things of God, than the Pharisees. Yet, they were the greatest opposers of the kingdom of God that Jesus had to face. Remember that the apostle Paul used to be a Pharisee and he was motivated by his zeal for God while he was persecuting the church.

Third, phariseeism seeks to have us serve the Lord in order to gain His approval, rather than living from the position of having our approval through the cross. The religious spirit tends to base relationship with God on personal discipline rather than the finished work of Christ. The motivation for this focus can be either fear or pride, or a combination of both. This does not imply that we would not do things to please the Lord, but our motive must remain on God—to be pleasing the Lord for His joy, not for our acceptance. One is God-centered, and the other is self-centered.

Here are some questions to help you discern whether or not you have the religious spirit: Does spending time basking in the love of God in personal communion make you antsy because you think you need to be doing something for the Lord? Do you have a hard time joining a church that you do not see as being perfect or near perfect? Do you do things in the church to be noticed by other people? Do you have an overwhelming guilt that you can never measure up to the Lord's standards? Are you prone to see more of what is wrong with other people and other churches than what is right with them? Do you believe that you have been appointed to fix everyone else? If you answered yes to any of these questions you are probably functioning out of a religious spirit. If so pray this prayer with me now:

Prayer

Lord, I repent of all phariseeism now. I ask you to bring the structure of the religious spirit to death at the cross of Christ. I see that my religious striving is sin and I turn my heart to Your grace. It is only by Your grace that I am saved and it is only by the power of the Holy Spirit that I can live the Christian life. Forgive me Lord, for trying to obey Your commandments in the power of my own strength, in Jesus' name, Amen.

12

Self-pity, Double-mindedness

Merriam-Webster's Online Dictionary defines self-pity as "a self-indulgent dwelling on one's own sorrows or misfortunes." Henry Wright, of Be in Health Ministries, describes self-pity as "the super glue that holds you to your past." I have personally found it to be a very strong and evil spirit in that it not only robs you of your joy but also locks in the valueless spirit so that you can't believe what God says about you in order to receive your inner healing. If you are going to get free of the valueless spirit you must make sure you have dealt decisively with self-pity.

I heard a pastor jokingly say one time that the problem with his pity parties is that he can't get anybody to attend. The truth is, however, that we do like to tell others about our story of awful circumstances in order to provoke the other person's sympathy. I rarely hear anyone come right out and say they are feeling sorry for themselves because that would defeat the purpose. The spirit of self-pity desires others to join us or collude. Collusion in self-pity is like forming an unholy alliance together. When someone approves of our self-pity it is like forming a conspiracy with that person.

This is because our self-pity needs to be fed in order to continue to maintain its hold. It requires complicity and agreement, both from us and others, in order to stay alive. When we can get someone to concur with us, it feeds our sense of self-pity, keeping us in bondage.

Self-pity is the strongest indication of a mind completely misdirected. God never planned our thoughts to be focused on ourselves except for those relatively brief periods when the Divine spotlight shines on our inner issues so that we might be whole. I know a woman who was one of the most miserable individuals I have ever met. She complained to everyone who would listen to her about how poorly she felt physically and how disappointing life had been for her. Her acquaintances began to feel that it was a "downer" just to be around her. Then one day she volunteered to help with the children's ministry of our church. When she began to pour out her life into serving the children she was the happiest I've ever seen her. In fact, her countenance took on a new radiant glow. When she took her focus off herself she felt joy and fulfillment. For her, self-pity became a deeply entrenched habit and she failed to realize that she had fallen into this pit.

In addition to robbing us of joy, self-pity often masks our deeper issues, keeping us trapped within a vicious cycle of hopelessness, rather than seeking to discover what our pain is showing us. When we develop the habit of feeling sorry for ourselves we prevent ourselves from taking positive action. Helen Keller aptly said, "Self-pity is our worst enemy and if we yield to it, we can never do anything wise in this world."

To experience freedom from self-pity requires a willingness to change. Once we understand the insidious character of this spirit, hopefully, we will engage our will, doing all that it takes, cooperating with the Holy Spirit to overcome it. We must recognize that our self-pity has become a patterned response to mask deeper issues in our lives.

I'm a strong advocate of journaling because once we write down our secret thoughts and feelings it helps us get a clearer view of how to proceed. I encourage you to write down in your journal, "I feel sorry for myself because..." And then fill in the blank. Write down as much as you can then put the list aside for a while. Set aside some time to meet with God. With journal and pen in hand, go to a place where you can still yourself in the presence of God. Get alone, away from screaming kids, telephones and traffic. I find that sitting in my back yard looking at the flowers and trees helps me get in a more contemplative state of mind. Sitting in your most comfortable chair or recliner and listening to soft worshipful music may also be helpful. Then write down these words, "Lord, what do You want to say to me regarding my thoughts and reasons for self-pity?"

Then fix your eyes on Jesus. One way to do this is to turn in your Bible to a familiar Gospel story and see the story played out in your mind's eye. Breathe deeply and slowly from your diaphragm and with your thoughts on Jesus listening to what you sense the Holy Spirit is telling you. His thoughts will always be life-giving, not judgmental or condemnatory. Write these thoughts down in your journal. Share what you have written with a trusted spiritual adviser for feedback.

In addition to journaling make sure to maintain an attitude of gratitude. Dr. David H. Fink, a psychiatrist for the veteran's administration wrote an article. 10,000 mentally ill patients were studied and it was found that they all had one thing in common: they were plagued with negative, critical, accusatory thoughts. Mark Virkler, author of numerous Christian books and a conference leader, did an inventory on himself years ago and he found to his chagrin that 80 percent of his thoughts were negative and accusatory in nature. I don't know what percentage of your thoughts is negative but I have found that you can't just rid your mind of negativity unless you fill it with positive thoughts. Peter Benenson said, "It is easier to light a candle than it is to curse the darkness." The apostle Paul said,

Finally, brothers, whatever is true, whatever is honorable, whatever is just, whatever is pure, whatever is lovely, whatever is commendable, if there is any excellence, if there is anything worthy of praise, think about these things.

(Philippians 4:8, ESV)

Many of us need a miracle from the hand of Almighty God but our attitude tends to block His intervention. A cursory glance at the Old Testament reveals how the Children of Israel were always murmuring and complaining. God wanted more for them but they shut down God's powerful acts by their attitude.

A glass of water can be half empty or half full. There are way too many negative thinkers. There is too much stinkin' thinkin'. Two girls gather grapes; one is happy because they have found grapes, and the other is unhappy because the grapes have seeds in them. Two women examine a bush, one is unhappy because it has thorns, and the other notices roses and is overjoyed by their fragrance. Two people are on vacation. One is happy because they still have another week of vacation. The other is unhappy because their vacation is half over. We see exactly what we train ourselves to see in this life. Our outlook on life is all-important and it is something we decide. Let me encourage you to practice giving thanks to God in everything.

In everything give thanks for this is the will of God in Christ Jesus concerning you.

(1 Thess. 5:18, KJV)

Steps to Overcoming Self-pity

1. A willingness to change.

2. Journal /reflection exercise (see below OR see next page).

3. Maintain an attitude of gratitude.

4. Confess and repent of all self-pity (including all negative, self-focused thinking). Confession and repentance takes legal ground away from the enemy.

Prayer

> *Lord, I confess and repent of the sin of self-pity. I have been focusing on myself rather than on You and other people. I repent for trying to get others to join me in feeling sorry for myself. My self-pity has been masking what You have been trying to show me and I confess that as sin. Lord, I ask You to bring to death at the cross all fleshly tendencies and structures in me that choose self-pity. Thank You for Your forgiveness and cleansing, in Jesus Name, Amen.*

Now make this declaration. *"Self-pity, in Jesus' Name, I reject you, I renounce you, and I break all agreements I ever made with you. I command you to leave me now and go to the place assigned you by Christ Jesus!"*

Journal Exercise

1. I feel sorry for myself because ...

_____

_____

_____

_____

_____

[Write down as much as you can then put the list aside for a while.]

2. Set aside time to meet with God. With journal and pen in hand, go to a place where you can still yourself in the presence of God. Ask God/write down these words, "Lord, what do You want to say to me regarding my thoughts and reasons for self-pity?"

3. Fix your eyes/thoughts on Jesus. One way to do this is to turn in your Bible to a familiar Gospel story and visualize the story in your mind's eye. Breathe deeply and slowly from your diaphragm and with your thoughts on Jesus, listen to what you sense the Holy Spirit is telling you. His thoughts will always be life-giving, not judgmental or condemnatory.

4. Write these thoughts down in your journal.

5. Share what you have written with a trusted spiritual adviser for feedback.

Double-mindedness

Most of us battle double-mindedness from time to time but the valueless spirit often leads to a struggle with uncertainty about what is right and what is wrong.   The Greek word translated "double minded" literally means "two-souled" or "two-minded."

Double-minded Christians wrestle with opposing desires. James says, *A double minded man is unstable in all his ways (James 1:8,* KJV). Look at a couple of other translations to get a fuller meaning: The New Living Translation says, *Their loyalty is divided between God and the world, and they are unstable in everything they do.* The Weymouth New Testament reads, *Such a one is a man of two minds, undecided in every step he takes.* A double-minded person shows indecision, vacillating between two opinions, and they feel unsure of themselves.

Double-minded people have difficulty receiving from the Lord. Back up a little bit in that James passage to verses 5-7. *If any of you lacks wisdom, let him ask God, who gives generously to all without reproach, and it will be given him. ⁶But let him ask in faith, with no doubting, for the one who doubts is like a wave of the sea that is driven and tossed by the wind. ⁷For that person must not suppose that he will receive anything from the Lord; ⁸he is a double-minded man, unstable in all his ways* (ESV).

As I stated earlier, the valueless spirit causes a person to doubt the goodness of God. If he believes that God is not good, why would he trust Him to give him the things he so desperately needs? Part of his mind believes God will answer his prayer but another part of his mind doesn't think God will be there for him. Doubt short-circuits our ability to receive from the Lord.

Double-minded people have a hard time keeping God's commandments. This is because they are facing two directions at the same time. James also says, *Draw near to God, and he will draw near to you. Cleanse your hands, you sinners, and purify your hearts, you double-minded* (James 4:8, ESV).

Double-mindedness keeps people locked into certain sins. Jesus never used the specific word "double-minded" but the concept was something He definitely warned against. For instance, consider Luke 16:13, *"No servant can serve two masters, for either he will hate the one and love the other, or he will be devoted to the one and despise the other. You cannot serve God and money"* (ESV). You can't face two directions simultaneously and please God.

Lot, Abraham's nephew, chose to live among the ungodly in Sodom probably because he loved money and prominence. He wanted to serve God but he also wanted to enjoy the pleasures of this world. He chose to live in the plain bordering the depraved cities of Sodom and Gomorrah. (See Genesis 13:1-13). Shortly after moving there he decided to live in the city itself and became a part of its culture serving as an official at the city gate. He believed in God but he didn't seem to have much of a spiritual impact on the citizens of that city. Double-mindedness brings spiritual powerlessness.

Another example of double-mindedness is what had happened to Israel during the reign of King Ahab. On Mt. Carmel Elijah approached the people and said,

> *"How long will you go limping between two different opinions? If the LORD is God, follow him; but if Baal, then follow him." And the people did not answer him a word.*
>
> (1 Kings 18:21, ESV)

The Children of Israel followed the king into the worship of Baal but, at the same time, they loved Yahweh. They were double-minded and could not make up their mind between God and Baal.

Double-mindedness causes Christians to try to split their energies between the world's system and the Kingdom of God. Jesus said, *"Whoever is not with me is against me, and whoever does not gather with me scatters"* (Luke 11:23, ESV). James exhorts us to stop vacillating between two allegiances. *You adulterous people! Do you not know that friendship with the world is enmity with God? Therefore whoever wishes to be a friend of the world makes himself an enemy of God* (James 4:4, ESV).

Prayer

Lord, I confess and repent of the sin of double-mindedness. I ask You to bring this tendency to death at the cross of Christ and give me a single-minded devotion so that I can serve You with all my heart, in Jesus' name, Amen.

13

Guilt and Shame

And Jesus saith unto them, All ye shall be offended because of me this night: for it is written, I will smite the shepherd, and the sheep shall be scattered. But after that I am risen, I will go before you into Galilee. But Peter said unto him, Although all shall be offended, yet will not I. And Jesus saith unto him, Verily I say unto thee, That this day, even in this night, before the cock crow twice, thou shalt deny me thrice. But he spake the more vehemently, If I should die with thee, I will not deny thee in any wise. Likewise also said they all. And they came to a place which was named Gethsemane:

And immediately, while he yet spake, cometh Judas, one of the twelve, and with him a great multitude with swords and staves, from the chief priests and the scribes and the elders. And he that betrayed him had given them a token, saying, Whomsoever I shall kiss, that same is he; take him, and lead him away safely. And as soon as he was come, he goeth straightway to him, and saith, Master, master; and kissed him. And they laid their hands on him, and took him. And one of them that stood by drew a sword, and smote a servant of the high priest, and cut off his ear. And Jesus answered and said unto them, Are ye come out, as against a thief, with swords and with staves to take me? I was daily with you in the temple teaching, and ye took me not: but the scriptures must be fulfilled. And they all forsook him, and fled. And there followed him a certain young man, having a linen cloth cast about his naked body; and the young men laid hold on him: And he left the linen cloth, and fled from them naked.

And as Peter was beneath in the palace, there cometh one of the maids of the high priest: And when she saw Peter warming himself, she looked upon him, and said, And thou also wast with Jesus of Nazareth. But he denied, saying, I know not, neither understand I what thou sayest. And he went out into the porch; and the cock crew. And a maid saw him again, and began to say to them that stood by, This is one of them. And he denied it again. And a little after, they that stood by said again to Peter, Surely thou art one of them: for thou art a Galilaean, and thy speech agreeth thereto. But he began to curse and to swear, saying, I know not this man of whom ye speak. And the second time the cock crew. And Peter called to mind the word that Jesus said unto him, Before the cock crow twice, thou shalt deny me thrice. And when he thought thereon, he wept.

(Mark 14:27-32, 43-52, 66-72, KJV)

These Scripture passages from Mark's Gospel deal with two individuals who were filled with guilt and shame – Peter and Judas. Although closely related, some people confuse guilt and shame. We feel guilty for what we DO. We feel shame for who we ARE. A person feels guilt for something he DID wrong. A person feels shame because he IS something wrong. We feel guilty because we lied to our mother or wife but we feel shame because we are not the person our mother or wife wants us to be. We feel embarrassed because we LOOK BAD but we feel shame because we think we ARE BAD. We need to separate the two. We feel shame because we see our self as flawed or a bad person.

Shame has no intelligence. It does not reason with us. It is a feeling. However, when we feel shame, it sets us at a cross roads. We have to choose: do we rush to get relief or do we first seek to find what caused the pain?

Reflect on the Fall that took place in the Garden of Eden. Consider Adam and Eve's awareness that their nakedness, their exposure to one another, created a feeling of insecurity, of threat, of shame. This demonstrates a basic component of shame. As shame came to the first couple, they became self-focused. Previously they had been God-focused. When God asked Adam, "Where are you?" He was not seeking information. He was giving him a chance to repent of his sin. Because Adam had now become self-focused, he immediately blamed God and the woman God had given him. Shame is often based on the fear that if people truly see who we are they will not accept us or love us and that ultimately they will abandon us. A pervasive fear of being exposed comes close to the heart of shame, that our very presence will evoke mocking or disgust.[xxv]

We live in a shame-based society. We sometimes say to children, "Shame on you!" Or to an adult, "Have you no shame?" Mark Twain put it bluntly: "Man is the only animal that blushes—or needs to." All normal people have felt shame. Webster defines shame as a painful emotion caused by consciousness of guilt, short coming, or impropriety; a condition of humiliating disgrace or disrepute; something that brings strong regret, censure, or reproach.

Shame can come in a lot of different ways, not just through some-thing you've done wrong. When I went to elementary school, I suffered strong feelings of shame. Because our family was so poor, I had to wear hand-me-downs. My mother did the best she could, but I was humiliated because of my appearance. As I went through those early years of school we couldn't afford "stylish" clothes. I never owned a pair of Levi Jeans, because they cost more than the other brands.

One lady came to the ministry I work with because she could never be truthful about her feelings with her husband. (This is public knowledge.) This caused trouble in the family. She told us that when she was a little girl about five or six years old, she had a doll that she greatly loved. One day, a neighbor's child grabbed it from her and savagely tore it apart. Being devastated, she ran home sobbing to her mother and sister and told them the story. Her mother said to her, "Why are you crying and carrying on so much? It's only a doll. You need to grow up. Stop this nonsense right now." Her mother shamed her for feeling grief and pain.[xxvi]

As she grew up, each time she felt grief or emotional pain, she also felt shame. So we ministered to her and asked Jesus to heal her of a heart broken over that childhood doll. Now she can grieve and not feel ashamed.

Sometimes when we sin shame sets in. There is a hopelessness that comes in from the belief that "I am no longer useful to God. I have sinned so badly that He will not forgive me and no longer loves me." Some time ago there was a young foreign student who flunked out at the University of Michigan. In shame he decided to disappear. For the next four years he hid in the unused attic of an Ann Arbor church. Taking great pains to conceal himself, he qui-etly prowled around only at night, living off food and water from the kitchen. He never left the building or spoke to a soul. No one ever suspected he was there. Then one day a slight mistake gave him away. The young recluse accidentally made some noise, the police were called, and he was finally discovered.

In a way that poor dropout is like many believers who are ashamed because of spiritual defeat. Overwhelmed by a sense of failure or embarrassment, they hesitate to take a stand for Christ and may even try to conceal the fact that they are Christians. Such lack of courage renders them useless to the cause of Christ and deprives them of the joy of sharing their faith with others.

Regret and shame are closely related. We feel regret over hasty decisions and lost opportunities. A man who gave up the chance to play professional baseball to enter Christian ministry tells how he used to struggle with bouts of depression and anger. He finally realized that what was bothering him was regret over his hasty decision and lost opportunities. Through a two-year in-depth Bible study on regret, he gained some practical insights for how to cope with the joylessness that comes from focusing on what might have been. Regret stems from disappointment in the decisions we've made.

A letter read in part: "Will you please help me? The agony I feel in my conscience is like an awful grinding, grinding, as I reap the results of my wasted years. I became a Christian at an early age, but later because I was told I was attractive and had a natural singing voice, I took a job in a nightclub. At 17 I married a man I met there. Christian friends urged me to use my talents for Christ, but I ignored them. I now have a girl 14 years old with an incurable disease. And listen, she has never been to church! God seems so far away, and I don't know how to reach my daughter. Please help me stop the terrible grinding of remorse!" The letter was signed, "A Brokenhearted Mother."

I'm sure Peter felt that way. He probably said to himself, "Why did I deny the Master? I am a failure. God can never use me. I'm just going to get out of God's work and go back to fishing." He was filled with shame. Shame also overtook Judas but for him it got to the point that he gave up all hope so he went out and hanged himself.

Shame keeps an individual locked into the past so that they cannot move on in the freedom that God has provided through the finished work of Christ on the cross. I have ministered to many people who were struggling with sexual bondages. No matter how hard we prayed and commanded the sexual demons to leave nothing happened until we stopped to deal with the issue of shame. Once we dealt with shame it was relatively easy to get the person free.

Here are three things we need to do to move beyond shame:

Receive God's Forgiveness

Dan Schaeffer tells this story of what happened a number of years ago in a small town in Spain. A man and his teenage son had an argument. The falling out led to deep feelings of bitterness and unforgiveness on both sides. The son soon left for the city. The father regretted the way he had treated his son and began to search for him. After several months, he still had not been able to locate the young man. Finally, as a last ditch effort, he placed the following ad in the classified section of a Madrid newspaper: "Dear Paco, meet me in front of the newspaper office at noon. All is forgiven. I love you. Your father." By twelve o'clock the next day, there were over 800 men named Paco gathered outside the newspaper building. Every one of them was looking for forgiveness from his father.[xvii]

There is a true guilt and a false guilt. How do we get healed of true guilt? Repent. Repentance is not something negative. True repentance is the foundation for change. We need to celebrate repentance. 1 John 1:9 says, *If we confess our sins he is faithful and just to forgive us our sins, and to cleanse us from all unrighteousness.* Did you know that God, after all He allowed His Son, Jesus, to go through on the cross, would be unjust if He wouldn't forgive you?

Forgive Yourself

Mentally arguing with yourself and rehashing the past doesn't solve anything. It just keeps you feeling sorry for yourself. Joseph's brothers had experienced this regret all their lives. When they were young men, motivated by jealousy, they sold their younger brother into slavery. Many years later their conversation reveals that they deeply regretted their misdeed.

> *And they said one to another, We are verily guilty concerning our brother, in that we saw the anguish of his soul, when he besought us, and we would not hear; therefore is this distress come upon us.* *[22]And Reuben answered them, saying, Spake I not unto you, saying, Do not sin against the child; and ye would not hear? therefore, behold, also his blood is required.*
>
> (Genesis 42:21-22, KJV)

Webster's defines remorse as a gnawing distress arising from a sense of guilt for past wrongs: SELF-REPROACH. The etymology of the word is to "bite again." After the Civil War, a woman entertained the distinguished Robert E. Lee in her home. She pointed out a once-beautiful oak tree that had been burned and disfigured by invading armies. "What should I do?" she asked with bitterness in her voice. "Cut it down and forget it," the general replied. That same advice applies to letting go of past pain.

Don't allow yourself to live in the past. Surrender your painful memories and experiences, and with a decisive act of your will, get on with your life.[xxviii]

Philippians 3:13-15 reads, *Brethren, I count not myself to have apprehended: but this one thing I do, forgetting those things which are behind, and reaching forth unto those things which are before, I press toward the mark for the prize of the high calling of God in Christ Jesus. Let us therefore, as many as be perfect, be thus minded: and if in anything ye be otherwise minded, God shall reveal even this unto you* (KJV).

You need to cut yourself some slack. Don't expect too much of yourself. Remember, you are but dust. Scripture says that we have this "treasure in earthern vessels." *But we have this treasure in earthen vessels, that the excellency of the power may be of God and not of us* (2 Corinthians 4:7, KJV).

Let Jesus Heal your Heart of the Inner Wound

Read about Peter's experience in John chapter 21. There you will see him early in the morning, around a charcoal fire, making 3 confessions. Jesus led Peter to an experience whereby he would receive inner healing. Know that Jesus wants to heal your broken heart and He will if you let Him.

Shame is a major motivator for many people. We should be motivated by hope rather than guilt and shame. Mark and Patti Virkler define hope as, "the confident expectation of good."[xxix]

Prayer for those Afflicted with Shame

Here is a prayer that Vision Life Ministries uses to help people who are suffering with shame:

Heavenly Father, I confess that I have sinned. I have accused you falsely. I have believed my own feelings and emotions and have exalted them above your Word. I have chosen to hide in the stronghold of shame rather than fellowship with you. I have made false gods of my own thoughts and have bowed down to worship them. By my attitudes and my actions, I have called you a liar. I have rejected your Word. I have rejected your love. I have rejected your grace. I have rejected your forgiveness. I repent of my unbelief. I change my mind. I choose to believe you. I choose to believe that whatever you say is the Truth. Lord Jesus, you said you are the Truth. Reveal yourself in me. Lord Jesus, I thank you that you took all these sins upon yourself on the cross. Father, forgive me and cleanse me. I accept the blood of your son, Jesus, as full payment for all my sins. Thank you for cleansing me from all unrighteousness, in Jesus' Name, Amen.

Prayer to Forgive Yourself

Here is a prayer that Vision Life Ministries uses to help people forgive themselves:

Heavenly Father, I forgive myself from my heart for all the things I have done wrong. (Tell God what those things are that you hold against yourself—those things that make you angry at yourself.) I let myself go free. I lay nothing to my charge. I require nothing of myself. I release myself into Your hands, Father, for you to get vengeance as You so choose. (Not that you are asking God to get vengeance on yourself, but that you are taking your hands off of the right to take vengeance. That right belongs to God alone.) I forgive myself from my heart for all the things I've done just because You, Heavenly Father, have already forgiven me. Now I release blessings to myself. Please make me a blessing to myself, in Jesus' Name, Amen.

(For a more thorough discussion on shame I highly recommend the book *Shame: Identity Thief,* by Dr. Henry Malone.)

Note: Permission is given to duplicate the following two worksheets for the purpose of ministering to individuals. These copies are not to be sold or mass produced without the publisher's permission.

14

Worksheets

The Valueless Strongman's Lies

(Check the lies/expectations you have believed. Place an asterisk next to four or five lies that are especially strong.)

__"If I perform well I will be loved and accepted."
__"Something is wrong with me."
__"My worth is in what I do."
__"I must reject others before they will reject me."
__"I'll never get anything right."
__"I'm a burden."
__"I am alone."
__"I'm an intrusion."
__"I have to depend on myself."
__"No one cares how I feel."
__"It's my fault my parents divorced or died."
__"No one will listen to me."
__"I'm the reason my parents can't get along."

__"No one will support me."

__"I don't belong."

__"No one will love me just for who I am."

__"I am a bad person."

__"If I isolate myself I won't get hurt."

__"I'm a mistake."

__"My best effort is never good enough."

__"I am unattractive."

__"I will never change into God's design for my life."

__"I will always be by myself."

__"If I avoid conflict I won't be rejected."

__"No one will protect me."

__"No one will help me."

__"I'm not lovable."

__"I'm not as good as everyone else."

__"I am inadequate."

__"God won't protect me."

__"Anything that is given to me will be taken away."

__"You can't trust God."

__"I must be what others want me to be."

__"If I'm invisible I won't be hurt."

__"Girls/boys aren't important."

__"The only thing I'm good for is sex."

__"My gifts and talents are inferior to others."

__"It would be better if I were dead."

__"I am not wanted."

__"I will always be abandoned."

__"I will always be left out."

__"No one will mentor me."

__"My actions will never be appreciated."

__"I am doomed to fail."

__"I am of no value/I am worthless."

__"I will never get ahead."

__"Everything I cherish will be taken from me."

__"I hate myself."

__"I will always struggle financially."
__"I'm a loser."
__"What I have to say is of no value."
__"God is not good."
__"I am invisible."
__"I am stupid."
__"I am rejected."
__"I am a failure."
__"God doesn't have a good plan for my life."
__"I was born the wrong sex."
__"I don't fit in."
__"I will be treated unjustly." *
__"I will be displaced."*
__"I won't let others know the real me or else they will reject me."

List other lies or ungodly expectations.

*(Note: If your ancestors were Native American these two expectations with asterisks are passed onto you through your DNA but they are not limited to those with a Native American heritage. Other people-groups have suffered similar fates.)

Subsidiary Valueless spirits
(Check all that apply).

__Undesirable
__Insignificance
__Unimportance
__Unnecessary
__Uselessness
__Invisible (Do you often feel unnoticed?)

__Unappreciated
__Self-pity
__Shame
__Defilement (Do you feel dirty because of past sin?)
__Disgrace
__Doomed to fail
__Victim spirit
__Broken heart spirit (keeps the heart from getting healed from past emotional trauma)
__Moodiness
__Sullenness (Are you usually gloomy?)

__Self-loathing (Do you hate yourself?)
__Rejection of self
__Disdain or scorn of self
__Accusation of self (Do you blame yourself?)
__Condemnation of self
__Ridicule of self
__Degradation of self (Do you put yourself down?)
__Spirit of poverty

__Abandonment
__Fear of abandonment
__Orphan spirit
__Ostracism
__Desertion
__Being and feeling left out
__Loneliness
__Isolation
__Division
__Separation
__Betrayal
__Illegitimacy

__Destruction of self (destructive behavior)
__Eradication of self (suicidal thought/attempts)
__Torture of self
__Insecurity
__Fear that others will reject you
__Fear of letting yourself be loved and/or loving others

__Damage to self (Cutting, accident prone, etc.)
__Self-sabotage

__Desire to punish self
__Rejection

__False humility
__Pride
__Unworthy
__Self-promotion
__Self-focus (Do you make an idol of yourself?)
__False piety (Do you need to show others how spiritual you are?)
__Religious spirit
__Self-deception (Are you easily deceived?)

__Self-doubt
__Self-questioning
__Lack of confidence
__Self-comparison
__Self-consciousness
__Placater (Do you always go along with what others want?)
__Chameleon spirit (changes personality and behavior to blend in with the expectations and desires of those he/she is presently with)
__Inordinate need to say something funny
__Attention-getting
__Excessive talking
__Double-mindedness

__Bitterness directed toward self
__Unforgiveness toward self
__Resentment turned inward
__Desire to harm self
__Anger at self

__Search for approval
__Perfectionism
__Performance (Do you have to perform to feel accepted?)
__Quest for legitimacy
__Drivenness

__Jealousy/Envy
__Anger at God and others
__Rebellion
__Covetousness

__Sexual immorality

__Adultery

__Pornography

__Addictions (Addictions often flow out of the valueless spirit and related inner pain)

15

Dismantling the Valueless
Strongman

The basic lie behind this spirit is "I am of no value."

Note: this is an antichrist spirit because it contravenes the great value God places in us as demonstrated by Christ's sacrificial death on the cross.

As they tell their story the prayer minister can begin to discern that this strongman is present. It is often received in the womb. Here are the steps to dismantling this strongman:

1. Repent of all related lies and judgments. Give them the *Valueless Strongman's Lies Worksheet*. Ask them to check off any lies they have believed and to put an asterisk by four or five that are especially strong.

Have them repent and renounce the lies they checked off using the following prayer model. It is very important to say these lies out loud. Then go back and lead them to repent and renounce individually the core lies, the ones with the asterisks. All the lies they believed can be dealt with as a group but the core lies should be addressed individually.

The recipient prays;

I repent for believing the lie that _____.

I confess the sin of my ancestors for having believed this lie.

I forgive _____ (usually dad and mom) and my other ancestors for their contribution to my receiving this lie.

I forgive myself for believing this lie.

I repent for my judgments against _____ and of all judgments against You God for allowing this to happen in my life.

I repent of that judgment and inner vow.

I receive Your forgiveness and I forgive myself for judging You and others.

I renounce the lie of _____ in my life and in the lives of my generations past.

After renouncing and repenting of all the applicable subsidiary lies, make sure that they repent and renounce the main lie that they are of no value or that they are worthless ("valueless" and "worthless" are synonymous).

2. Give the recipient a pen and a piece of paper. Instruct them to close their eyes and tune to the flow of the Holy Spirit. (It may be helpful to play soft worshipful music in the back-

ground.) Instruct them to relax and focus their eyes on Jesus.

It often helps to recall a Gospel story visualizing Jesus in their mind's eye in that Scripture passage. Scripture tells us to "fix our eyes on Jesus" (Hebrews 12:2).

After they still themselves in this manner, have them ask the Lord what He wants to say regarding each lie that they indicated was especially strong.

They must write this down, "Lord, what do you want to say to me regarding the lie that _____."

After they tell you what they sense God is saying, ask them to write down the following confession: "Regarding the lie that _____, I confess the opposite divine truth that _____."

They must write down on a piece of paper the lie along with the countering divine truth to aid them in remembering what The Holy Spirit said to them. Give them the homework assignment to declare this confession out loud every day for at least 30 days.

> Note: if the person is struggling with hearing God's voice skip this part and move on.

Encourage them to read *4 Keys to Hearing God's Voice,* by Mark & Patti Virkler. They may also go to www.CWGMinistries.org to receive free streaming audio and video tracts on How to Hear God's Voice. In addition, instruct them to repeat the Vision Life Ministries *My Declaration of Faith* assignment for 30 days (See appendix) if they have not already done so after a previous ministry session.

3. Give them the *Valueless Strongman Underlings Worksheet*. Tell the recipient to mark all that apply. Explain that some of these underlings may not be evident in them but they run in their bloodline because they are evident in mom, dad, or grandparents.

The minister says, "In the name of Jesus I bind the valueless strongman."

Then go through the ones they checked off. Have them repeat after you, "I reject, renounce and break every agreement I ever made with _____ and I command you to leave me now and never return, in Jesus' name." (I usually have them repeat this renunciation for each grouping but name each one they checked off out loud.)

Then the minister addresses the underlings they marked off. Say something like this, "_____, I bind and break your power, I cancel your assignments, and I command you to go to dry places, in Jesus' name." (The exact wording is not as important as your authority in Christ.)

Listen to the Holy Spirit. For some of the underlings you may need to lead them to say, "I bring this fleshly tendency to death at the cross of Christ."

Remember, we're dealing with two issues, the flesh and evil spirits. You cannot cast out the flesh. You may need to have them repent for having come into agreement with any of these underlings which seem especially strong.

The underlings often get weaker and leave more easily as you work your way down the list. Some of these underlings are weak so you can name them individually and then command them to leave in groups. Others are strong and you will have to speak to them one at a time until they leave. Take your time, don't rush it, and rely on the Holy Spirit! Remember that repentance is a major weapon against the enemy's devices and they may need to repent of some of these underlings individually and in more depth.

4. Pull the iniquity of valuelessness up out of their body and mind and out of their DNA. This strongman programs the mind to think in accordance with the above list. Iniquity is different than sin. In the original language of the Bible they are two different and distinct words.

Iniquity can get passed on generationally by our ancestors and I like to refer to it as a spiritual DNA that makes us subject to certain unwanted propensities. (For more insight on this subject please read Ana Mendez Ferrell's book, *Iniquity,* E & A International Publishing.)

Ask God to cut off any valueless spirits coming from the second heaven and to close any portal of access. Then pray this: "In Jesus' Name I pull up the iniquity of valuelessness out of _____ (recipient's name)."

With the person's permission, lay hands on them and repeat the prayer until you get a peace or release in your spirit. Ask them if they are receiving any mental pictures because sometimes at this point the Holy Spirit reveals the entry point for the valueless spirit, either by what was done to the recipient or to someone in their generations past.

5. After going through the entire list, go back to the strongman and command it to leave along with all of its underlings named or unnamed. There may be other underlings not mentioned, but if you have cast out those listed above, the strongman will usually leave without a big fight because it has lost

most of its defensive armor. *Note: If you only lead them into the truth-encounter without casting out this spirit, the value-less spirit may remain in place and attempt to re-establish itself and vice versa.*

6. Heal the trauma. See the chapter in this book entitled "Steps to Healing the Trauma."

7. Almost always, the person who has been infected with the valueless strongman has also received the core lie which states, "God is not good." It is the same lie the devil foisted on Eve in the Garden of Eden. It's easy for the enemy to get us to move from, "I'm of no value" to "God is not good." He gets us to reason that if I'm of no value and God created me, then logically, God is not good.

Obviously, it is very difficult for us to trust God if, in our heart, we believe that He is not good. People with the valuelessness strongman usually have a hard time trusting God. I have rarely known it to be otherwise. This other lie and its dynamic needs to be brought out into the light so the recipient can receive a truth encounter. They need to forgive God and repent of all judgments against Him.

It is extremely important that our recipients learn to walk out their freedom. They need to bring every thought captive to the obedience of Christ and renew their minds. I recommend that they go over the above list a second time with the prayer minister in about two or three weeks.

16

Steps to Healing the Trauma

Whether you were an unwanted pregnancy, your parents wanted a boy/girl, you were the victim of childhood abuse, or harsh words were spoken over you, the resulting trauma is similar. Trauma gives the enemy an opening to insert the lie in our hearts that we are of little or no intrinsic value. In such cases it is natural to go through life as an adult feeling pervasive fear and helplessness regarding the circumstances you had no control over. The good news is that God offers ways to overcome the traumatic events of our past.

Here are some practical things you can do to facilitate your healing;

1. Recognize that the lies you received are the same lies countless multitudes of other people have believed. You are not alone. Others have been healed so why not you? In John 16:33 Jesus said, *"These things I have spoken to you, so that in Me you may have peace. In the world **you have** tribulation, but take courage; I have overcome the world"* (NASB, emphasis added). Most versions of the Bible mistranslate

this verse reading, "you **will have** tribulation," implying that some time in the future you will have tribulation, but not necessarily have it now. However, The word "have" (*exete*) is in the present tense in the original Greek language, not future. The word *thlipsis,* translated "tribulation," means pressure, affliction, anguish, burdened, persecution, tribulation and trouble. The Bible is saying that everybody experiences *thlipsis* from one degree to another right now. The reason for this is because we live in a fallen world and in a fallen world affliction comes on a regular basis. Take courage though, because Jesus has overcome this fallen world system.

2. Talk about the painful circumstances of your life with someone you trust to keep the information confidential. Share your thoughts, feelings, and your reactions to hurtful events in a safe environment. It is important to find someone who will really listen without judging you. You may need to seek out a professional licensed counselor with whom you can keep talking about your pain until you have no need to talk about it anymore. Keep in mind that Satan works in the hidden; God works in the light. Once we bring our memories out in the open the light of God can shine on them to bring direction and healing.

3. Get in touch with your emotions. Christians often learn to shut down their emotions because they believe that good godly people shouldn't feel that way. Read the Psalms and see how David expressed his emotions. He would pour out his complaint to God. When injustice has been done it is natural to feel angry. Tell God about it. He already knows what's in your heart and doesn't love you any less. He wants you to vocalize the anger to Him so that it can be released. Most people are angry at God and refuse to admit it for fear of judgment. Tell Him about your anger and disappointment. He won't judge you for it.

4. Remember that healing is usually a process, it is not instantaneous. The pain and trauma come off in layers, much like peeling an onion. Be patient with yourself because healing takes time. Sometimes you will feel like you're taking three steps forward and two steps backward so don't become discouraged and give up.

5. Look for the good in the midst of the negatives that happened to you. What have you learned as a result of the trauma? Romans 8:28, CEV says, *We know that God is always at work for the good of everyone who loves him. They are the ones God has chosen for his purpose.* God didn't cause your trauma but He can use it for His glory and your good. Your painful circumstances can make you a stronger and wiser person. The potential is there for you to learn and grow in ways not possible had the trauma never occurred.

6. Remember, that although you were victimized you don't have to remain a victim. You are not responsible for what was done to you but you are responsible for the way you respond to what was done to you. By following the principles outlined in this book you will emerge a victor.

The Prayer Minister

At the time of this writing I am an associate minister with Vision Life Ministries. VLM is dedicated to training people for a ministry of deliverance and inner healing. We don't do counseling per se, we are prayer ministers. I'm not a licensed counselor and don't want to be because we approach healing from a different perspective. (There is a legitimate place for professional counselors.) What counselors call "clients" we call "recipients" because we don't want our terminology to imply that we are doing counseling. (If you feel called to this type of ministry I encourage you to contact the VLM office and enroll in the extensive training events offered.)

According to the VLM model, the prayer minister invites the recipient to talk about their life in three stages – stage one, their life from when they were born to when they started school; stage two, their life during their school-age years; and stage three, their life as an adult. Ninety percent of a person's strongholds (system of lies) are formed in the first six years of life. We ask some probing questions such as, "Were you a wanted pregnancy? Did mom have a hard time carrying you? Was it a difficult birth process? When I say the word "dad," as a preschooler, what do feel? When I say the word "mom" what do you feel? What is your earliest memory, etc.?" It is extremely important to get the background information first before doing any deliverance and inner healing except in rare cases.

As the person tells their story we look for the traumatic issues of their life, taking brief notes so as not to forget important details. After the interview we begin by dealing with the open doors that gave Satan legal access into the person's life. Those doors are willful sin, unforgiveness, inner vows and judgments, curses, and trauma. We minister thoroughly in these areas to help the recipient remove the legal ground to the enemy's ability to afflict their life. Then we cast out the fourteen root spirits. Fourteen times in the Bible it specifically says, "the spirit of…" The root spirits are as follows: infirmity, divination, fear, bondage, whoredom/idolatry, haughtiness, antichrist, deaf and dumbness, error, sleep and slumber, jealousy, and lying.

During the initial session we deal with a significant level of trauma because it is one of the five doors. Dr. Henry Malone, founder of VLM, has developed a powerful method of pulling up the pain out of a person's heart. The prayer minister lays their hand over the recipient's heart. (If the recipient is a person of the opposite sex I ask my wife [or female assistant] to lay her hand on the individual's heart. I ask the recipient's permission to do so and at the same time ask if I can put my hand on top of the other female's hand.)

Then I ask the person to open up their heart to me. I pray, "Lord Jesus, I ask you to open _____'s heart. In Jesus' Name, I call up the pain in _____'s heart. I call up the pain. Come up pain. I speak to the deep, deep pain. Jesus, hold his/her pain." The prayer ministers take their time to allow the pain to come up. Tears often flow down the face of the recipient at this point in the healing process. Continue to work through other specific painful events in their life, pulling up the pain.

The first session lasts between four to six hours. Because of the length of the initial session I don't recommend dealing with the valueless spirit at this time, but wait and minister in this area during a follow-up session. If you try to do too much in the initial session both you and the recipient will be too exhausted to function effectively.

During the follow-up session go through the valueless spirit worksheets which help identify the lies and subsidiary spirits of the valueless strongman. Go through the process described in the chapter entitled "Dismantling the Valueless Strongman." Now you are ready to deal with trauma at a deeper level than what was done in the initial session. You may want to use the techniques in the following scenario, if led by the Spirit to do so.

"Brittney, I would like us to break all negative soul-ties you have with anyone the enemy used to bring trauma into your life. Some soul-ties are good and some are negative. For instance, the soul-tie you have with the man who molested you is ungodly and needs to be broken. (Soul ties should have been severed during the initial ministry session but you may uncover more during this follow-up. Break all negative soul-ties with anyone who victim-ized the person. Break *ungodly* soul ties between them and their parents if their parents are living. Break all soul ties if their parents are deceased.)

Do I have your permission?" (Wait for their permission to break these soul ties.) They may need more understanding on this subject before proceeding.

Chester and Betsy Kylstra define an ungodly soul tie as, "an un-godly covenant with another person, organization, or thing based on an unhealthy emotional and/or sexual relationship/attach-ment." "This covenant binds the two people together or it binds a person to an organization or thing." [xxx]

"Brittney, pray this prayer after me. 'Father God, please break my ungodly soul ties with _____.

I release myself from him and I release him from me. As I pray this Lord, I ask that You would cause him to be all that you want him to be and that you would cause me to be all that you want me to be.' [xxxi]

I forgive _____ for his involvement in forming this ungodly soul tie."

Minister prays: "In Jesus' name, I break the power of any evil spirit attempting to maintain this soul tie. Now I take my sword and I sever the ungodly soul tie between you and _____ (I use a symbolic hand motion as though I'm cutting it with a sword).

I pull up any of _____'s soul/spirit out of Brittney (Us-ing a prophetic hand motion I pull it up out of their heart) and send it back to where it belongs, and I call back any part of

Brittney that was stolen. I thank You Lord for restoring her soul to wholeness."

"Brittney, do I have your permission to take authority over your entire being in order to cut off some things that need to go? (Don't do this without their permission.) In the name of Jesus, I take authority over your being and command all the effects of everything you checked off on your worksheets, down to the cellular level, and all the results of trauma that led to believing the valueless lies to leave you now. I command the spirit of trauma to leave you now and go to dry places." (Keep commanding until you sense it leave.)

"I take authority over your body and command all the long-term and short-term effects of trauma to leave you now. I command it to leave without doing you harm or injury. I command all the effects of those harsh words, defiling touch, rejection, abandonment, betrayal, abuse, neglect, etc. (Name the specific trauma they mentioned in their interview) to leave you now."

"I bless your lymphatic system, endocrine system, your liver and other systems to safely eliminate any toxins which are by-products of trauma and the iniquity of valuelessness." (In cases where there has been defiling activity such as molestation, incest or severe abuse, it may be helpful to cast out of the body the memory of smells, feelings, tastes, sounds, and touch associated with the abuse.) [xxxii]

"Brittney, is it OK if I place my hands on your head?" (Get permission.) "Heavenly Father, I ask You to repair and restore Brittney's amygdala and her hippocampus." (The amygdala has been shown in research to perform a primary role in the processing and memory of emotional reactions. The hippocampus plays important roles inlong-term and spatial navigation.) Repair them so that her healing of trauma can progress rapidly.

"I command all spirits of fear to leave her hypothalamus, adrenal and all other glands now, in Jesus' name. I command all spirits of depression to leave her pineal gland now, in Jesus' name. I ask You Lord to re-establish the connection between the hemispheres of her brain." (Often extremely traumatized individuals live predominately out of the left hemisphere of their brain and need the right side to be stimulated so that they can be more balanced.)

"I ask You Lord to re-establish and synchronize both explicit and implicit memories and that You would reactivate any connections required for her to retrieve the memories needed to complete her healing." xxxiii

"Lord, I ask you to begin to dismantle all automatic human responses that developed as a result of her trauma, including all abnormal fright responses, triggers, fears and phobias."

"I ask You Lord to rebuild, re-establish, and re-create any electrical or chemical connections broken or improperly reconnected as a result of her trauma. I pray that she can operate within the normal limits of high and low stimuli and that she can remain in control emotionally when stimulus is high."xxxiv

"Father, I ask You to disconnect any evil entities coming from the second heaven against Brittney that have gained access through the traumatic events she suffered."

"I ask You to close any portals of access." Brittney, the Bible says in Psalm 115:16, *'The heavens are the LORD's heavens, but the earth he has given to the children of man'* (ESV). I don't believe that we have authority over second-heaven level entities. That's why we're asking God to deal with them. We have authority over earth-bound spirits but not high-level spirits which dwell in the second-heaven."

"In Jesus' name, I take authority over and cancel all assignments of familiar spirits made against Brittney as a result of her traumatic experiences."

"In Jesus' name, I pull the trauma up out of your DNA." (Don't rush this but wait until you get a peace or release that you are finished).

Through the eyes of my spirit I often see things leave the recipient that look like little spiral cork screws coming up and out. Sometimes in the process of pulling up this type of trauma the recipient sees a particular scene in their mind's eye. This scene depicts an event that happened, either in their life or in the life of an ancestor, that opened the door to trauma becoming programmed into their DNA. As you pray, ask the recipient what they sense or see.

"Heavenly Father, I ask you to cleanse Brittney's emotions and heal them so that they will be pleasing to You. In Jesus name, I command any demons afflicting her emotions to leave now and never return. I ask You Father to close all doorways through which the enemy gained access to her emotions by what was done to her and seal those doorways shut. I ask you to wash her emotions by the living waters of Your river."[xxxviii]

Spiritual Vision

Another, though somewhat controversial, way to facilitate healing from traumatic events is to see Jesus in the situation. I do not advocate what is called "guided imagery" where, in essence, you recreate the history of the recipient's life. I believe guided imagery is dangerous and must be avoided.

On the other hand, theologically, all Christians must agree that if He is God, Jesus is both omnipresent and transcends time. If this is true, then logically, Jesus was present with you when you experienced the trauma. I have discovered that when a person gets a glimpse of Jesus in their painful memory that healing almost automatically occurs.

Some ministers are reluctant to use this technique because, as I already mentioned, they want to avoid guided-imagery. Another concern is the fact that in a significant number of cases the recipient receives a vision of a false Jesus. The false Jesus takes them deeper into deception and bondage. For example, I asked Carla to look to see if she could see Jesus in a hurtful situation that had brought great damage in her life. She said, "Yes, I see Him." I asked, "What is He doing?" She answered, "He's watching me." I asked, "Now what is He doing?" "He just turned and walked away," she replied with a sad resignation in her voice. What Carla was seeing was a false Jesus. The true Jesus of Nazareth is full of compassion and deeply cares about the trials and tribulations of each and every human being.

Reggie clearly had the valueless strongman at work in his life. He came from an abusive background. I asked the Lord to take him to a scene from his past that opened the door to the worthlessness he felt. Immediately, a picture came into his mind of when he was about five or six years old. In this scene his mother was beating him in the stomach with her fists. His mother often beat him mercilessly. I asked Reggie to look with the eyes of his spirit to see where Jesus was. "Do you see Him?" "Yes, He's standing right beside my mother," he responded. "Can you see His face," I inquired. "Yes. His eyes are red and beady and He's staring at me," he said, somewhat surprised by the vision. Obviously Reggie was not seeing the true Jesus.

In cases where you suspect they are seeing a false Jesus, simply instruct the recipient to ask Jesus, "Are you the Jesus Christ that came in the flesh?" I led Reggie to do so and after he did I asked, "What is Jesus doing now?" "He instantly vanished," Reggie responded.

Scripture says;

> *Beloved, believe not every spirit, but try the spirits whether they are of God: because many false prophets are gone out into the world. Hereby know ye the Spirit of God: Every spirit that confesseth that Jesus Christ is come in the flesh is of God: And every spirit that confesseth not that Jesus Christ is come in the flesh is not of God: and this is that spirit of antichrist, whereof ye have heard that it should come; and even now already is it in the world.*
>
> (1 John 4:1-3, KJV)

The true Jesus is not afraid or ashamed to testify that He came in the flesh. A false Jesus will usually leave rather than answer this question.

The true Jesus will never contradict His Word. He will never act out of character to what is revealed about Him in Scripture. He doesn't uncover authority figures in your life. For example, the true Jesus you see in a vision will never tell you your father molested you if you have no conscious memory of that event. The true Jesus you see through the eyes of your heart will never speak to you in accusatory or condemnatory language.

Even still, if a false Jesus shows up in the memory it can be a learning experience.

Carla, in the above story had a false view of Jesus and a demon was lurking nearby seeking to take advantage of her ungodly belief. She believed God would abandon her just like her earthly father did. That's why when she saw Jesus in her memory He just turned and walked away. In his heart of hearts Reggie believed God was mean and cruel. The Jesus he saw looked evil. In situations like these a great opportunity exists to point out that they have a false view of God and to lead them into a truth encounter as to who God really is.

Remember, we're not trying to get Jesus to "show up" in a painful memory. We are simply using the eyes of our heart to see where Jesus actually was when the event occurred in the person's life. This is not guided imagery and it is not re-creating history.

Some people can't see anything through spiritual vision usually because they have not trained their senses to do so or because they have shut down the intuitive side of their brain. These people are often analytical and rely heavily on human reasoning. Sometimes they can't visualize due to the making of an inner vow regarding lust of the eyes. For instance, a man has a problem with sexual fantasy so he vows not to use his imagination; in which case the vow needs to be broken. An exercise I have found that helps stimulate my spiritual vision is to meditate on Scripture. As I read the Biblical stories I make it a practice to visualize the scenes through the eyes of my heart. Doing so also makes the Bible come alive. People who have trained their spiritual senses to see through the eyes of their heart make the job of the prayer minister a lot easier. However, if they can't see in the spirit there are other ways to facilitate healing.

Here is an example of seeing Jesus in a painful situation from my own life. One day I asked the Lord to show me what negative pictures of people or experiences I was holding in my heart which contributed to the heart problem of rejection. Immediately a scene came to mind of an incident years ago when I was in a restaurant with one of my deacons. At that time we had been meeting once a week for breakfast to talk about the affairs of the church. He presented himself as my supportive faithful friend and I believed that in him I had someone to confide in. The church was experiencing considerable division and as the senior pastor I was deeply distressed.

One day at breakfast I asked him about the cause of the church's problems. He proceeded to unload on me about what a bad pastor I was. I felt hurt, rejected and betrayed. (From that moment on he went on a crusade to stir others up and to get me fired.) Then in that vision I saw Jesus standing next to me where I was sitting in the booth. He put His hand on my shoulder and was looking sad. Then He pulled this 4 to 5-inch thorn out of my heart. It was bloody. He put His hand on my heart to pull out the poison and heal the wound. It made me feel loved and very peaceful. That vision of Jesus helped me receive significant healing from that painful experience of rejection and betrayal. I know He is always with me to heal my heart of every wound if I will let Him.

Closing Remarks

If you find that you are displaying symptoms of the valueless spirit, I pray that you will not simply read this book and then lay it aside on a shelf to collect dust. I hope that you have not been looking for a quick fix to rid your life of some of the garbage you've been struggling with. It took the enemy years to reinforce the valueless spirit's hold. First he planted a seed (a lie) and then he has been watering and nurturing it ever since so that its root system would run deep and become very difficult to dislodge.

Much is at stake. The valueless spirit's task is to make it so that you will always have problems truly living the abundant life Jesus said He came to give. You will find it difficult to trust God when you encounter pressure. And it will hinder your witness because others won't want what you have.

Therefore, I urge you to contend for your healing. Engage your will so that you fully cooperate with the Holy Spirit. Don't be passive because the passive Christian will remain in bondage. Go to a well-trained deliverance/inner healing minister and deal with your heart issues. Don't think that you can repair your woundedness all on your own—just you and God. God has designed the Body of Christ to be interdependent, not independent. We are often blinded to the real issues of our lives and it takes another person to look at our hearts with a different set of eyes.

Do the recommended exercises in this book. When I minster to people I usually give them a homework assignment. When I do a follow-up session with that same person I ask if they completed their assignment. If they tell me they have not, it communicates to me that they don't want it bad enough. If they really wanted to get healed they would put forth the necessary effort.

You may have setbacks but don't give up. You may feel that when you take three steps forward you take two steps backward. It's okay. Keep pressing on. Inner healing often happens in stages much like pealing an onion. If you are a true follower of Jesus Christ then the Holy Spirit, the Third Person of the Trinity, lives within you. This amazing truth means that you don't have to walk-out your freedom in the power of your own energy and determination. He is there inside you to help you do what you can't do in your own strength.

Appendix

Scripture Meditation to Overcome the Valueless Spirit

Speak the following verses out loud, addressing your human spirit. Your human spirit will hear the words coming out of your mouth and will be strengthened and blessed. To get the truths of these verses down in your spirit do this exercise every day for at least 30 days.

So God created man in his own image, in the image of God created he him; male and female created he them.
(Genesis 1:27, KJV)

So God created man in his own image, in the image of God he created him; male and female he created them.
(Genesis 1:27, ESV)

For the LORD'S portion is his people; Jacob is the lot of his inheritance. He found him in a desert land, and in the waste howling wilderness; he led him about, he instructed him, he kept him as the apple of his eye.

(Deuteronomy 32:9-10, KJV)

But the LORD's portion is his people, Jacob his allotted heritage. "He found him in a desert land, and in the howling waste of the wilderness; he encircled him, he cared for him, he kept him as the apple of his eye."

(Deuteronomy 32:9-10, ESV)

What is man, that thou art mindful of him? And the son of man, that thou visitest him? For thou hast made him a little lower than the angels, and hast crowned him with glory and honour. Thou madest him to have dominion over the works of thy hands; thou hast put all things under his feet:

(Psalm 8:4-6, KJV)

Then I ask, "Why do you care about us humans? Why are you concerned for us weaklings?" You made us a little lower than you yourself, [a] *and you have crowned us with glory and honor. You let us rule everything your hands have made. And you put all of it under our power--* **Footnotes:** *a. verse 5. you yourself: Or "the angels" or "the beings in heaven."*

(Psalm 8:4-6, CEV)

Like a father pitieth his children, so the LORD pitieth them that fear him.

(Psalm 103:13, KJV)

As a father shows compassion to his children, so the LORD shows compassion to those who fear him.

(Psalm 103:13, ESV)

I will praise thee: for I am fearfully and wonderfully made: marvelous are thy works; and that my soul knoweth right well. My substance was not hid from thee, when I was made in secret, and curiously wrought in the lowest parts of the earth. Thine eyes did see my substance, yet being unperfect; and in thy book all my members were written, which in continuance were fashioned, when as yet there was none of them. How precious also are thy thoughts unto me, O God! How great is the sum of them! If I should count them, they are more in number than the sand: when I awake, I am still with thee.

(Psalm 139: 14-18, KJV)

and I praise you because of the wonderful way you created me. Everything you do is marvelous! Of this I have no doubt. Nothing about me is hidden from you! I was secretly woven together deep in the earth below, but with your own eyes you saw my body being formed. Even before I was born, you had written in your book everything I would do. Your thoughts are far beyond my understanding, much more than I could ever imagine. I try to count your thoughts, but they outnumber the grains of sand on the beach. And when I awake, I will find you nearby.

(Psalm 139:14-18, CEV)

Can a woman forget her suckling child, that she should not have compassion on the son of her womb? Yea, they may forget, yet will I not forget thee. Behold, I have graven thee upon the palms of my hands; thy walls are continually before me.

(Isaiah 49:15-16, KJV)

The LORD answered, "Could a mother forget a child who nurses at her breast? Could she fail to love an infant who came from her own body? Even if a mother could forget, I will never forget you. A picture of your city is drawn on my hand. You are always in my thoughts!"

(Isaiah, 49:15-16, CEV)

For I know the thoughts that I think toward you, saith the LORD, thoughts of peace, and not of evil, to give you an expected end.

(Jeremiah 29:11, KJV)

I will bless you with a future filled with hope--a future of success, not of suffering.

(Jeremiah 29:11, CEV)

Before I formed thee in the belly I knew thee; and before thou camest forth out of the womb I sanctified thee, and I ordained thee a prophet unto the nations.

(Jeremiah 1:5, KJV)

"Jeremiah, I am your Creator, and before you were born, I chose you to speak for me to the nations."

(Jeremiah 1:5, CEV)

The LORD hath appeared of old unto me, saying, Yea, I have loved thee with an everlasting love: therefore with lovingkindness have I drawn thee.

(Jeremiah 31:3, KJV)

the LORD appeared to him from far away. I have loved you with an everlasting love; therefore I have continued my faithfulness to you.

(Jeremiah 31:3, ESV)

The LORD thy God in the midst of thee is mighty; he will save, he will rejoice over thee with joy; he will rest in his love, he will joy over thee with singing.

(Zephaniah 3:17, KJV)

The LORD your God is in your midst, a mighty one who will save; he will rejoice over you with gladness; he will quiet you by his love; he will exult over you with loud singing.

(Zephaniah 3:17, ESV)

For thus saith the LORD of hosts; After the glory hath he sent me unto the nations which spoiled you: for he that toucheth you toucheth the apple of his eye.

(Zechariah 2:8, KJV)

Then the glorious LORD All-Powerful ordered me to say to the nations that had raided and robbed Zion: Zion is as precious to the LORD as are his eyes. Whatever you do to Zion, you do to him.

(Zechariah 2:8, CEV)

And fear not them which kill the body. But are not able to kill the soul: but rather fear him which is able to destroy both soul and body in hell. Are not two sparrows sold for a farthing? And one of them shall not fall on the ground without your Father. But the very hairs of your head are all numbered. Fear ye not therefore, ye are of more value than many sparrows.

(Matthew 10:28-31, KJV)

Don't be afraid of people. They can kill you, but they cannot harm your soul. Instead, you should fear God who can destroy both your body and your soul in hell. Aren't two sparrows sold for only a penny? But your Father knows when any one of them falls to the ground. Even the hairs on your head are counted. So don't be afraid! You are worth much more than many sparrows.

(Matthew 10:28-31, CEV)

For God so loved the world, that he gave his only begotten Son, that whosoever believeth in him should not perish, but have everlasting life.

(John 3:16, KJV)

God loved the people of this world so much that he gave his only Son, so that everyone who has faith in him will have eternal life and never really die.

(John 3:16, CEV)

Ye have not chosen me, but I have chosen you, and ordained you, that ye should go and bring forth fruit, and that your fruit should remain: that whatsoever ye shall ask of the Father in my name, he may give it you.

(John 15:16, KJV)

You did not choose me. I chose you and sent you out to produce fruit, the kind of fruit that will last. Then my Father will give you whatever you ask for in my name.

(John 15:16, CEV)

At that day ye shall ask in my name: and I say not unto you, that I will pray the Father for you: For the Father himself loveth you, because ye have loved me, and have believed that I came out from God.

(John 16:26-27, KJV)

In that day you will ask in my name, and I do not say to you that I will ask the Father on your behalf; for the Father himself loves you, because you have loved me and have believed that I came from God.

(John 16:26-27, ESV)

For ye have not received the spirit of bondage again to fear; but ye have received the Spirit of adoption, whereby we cry, Abba, Father.

(Romans 8:15, KJV)

God's Spirit doesn't make us slaves who are afraid of him. Instead, we become his children and call him our Father.

(Romans 8:15, CEV)

What shall we then say to these things? If God be for us, who can be against us? He that spared not his own son, but delivered him up for us all, how shall he not with him also freely give us all things?

(Romans 8:31-32, KJV)

What can we say about all this? If God is on our side, can anyone be against us? God did not keep back his own Son, but he gave him for us. If God did this, won't he freely give us everything else ?

(Romans 8:31-32, CEV)

For he hath made him to be sin for us, who knew no sin; that we might be made the righteousness of God in him.

(2 Corinthians 5:21, KJV)

Christ never sinned! But God treated him as a sinner, so that Christ could make us acceptable to God.

(2 Corinthians 5:21, CEV)

And will be a Father unto you, and ye shall be my sons and daughters, saith the Lord Almighty.
(2 Corinthians 6:18, KJV)

and I will be a father to you, and you shall be sons and daughters to me, says the Lord Almighty.
(2 Corinthians 6:18, ESV)

Wherefore thou art no more a servant, but a son; and if a son, then an heir of God through Christ.
(Galatians 4:7, KJV)

You are no longer slaves. You are God's children, and you will be given what he has promised.
(Galatians 4:7, CEV)

For all the law is fulfilled in one word, even in this; Thou shalt love thy neighbor as thyself.
(Galatians 5:14, KJV)

All that the Law says can be summed up in the command to love others as much as you love yourself.
(Galatians 5:14, CEV)

According as he hath chosen us in him before the foundation of the world, that we should be holy and without blame before him in love: Having predestinated us unto the adoption of children by Jesus Christ to himself, according to the good pleasure of his will. To the praise of the glory of his grace, wherein, he hath made us accepted in the beloved.
(Ephesians 1:4-6, KJV)

Before the world was created, God had Christ choose us to live with him and to be his holy and innocent and lov-

ing people. God was kind and decided that Christ would choose us to be God's own adopted children. God was very kind to us because of the Son he dearly loves, and so we should praise God.

(Ephesians 1:4-6, CEV)

My Declaration of Faith

Make this declaration out loud every day for at least 30 days:

Heavenly Father, I choose to believe what your Word says about me (Isaiah 40:8) rather than my carnal thoughts and feelings (2 Cor. 10:4). My unbelief has been sin (Rom. 14:23).

Lord Jesus, thank you for loving me enough to die on the cross for my sins (Rom. 5:8).

There is, therefore, now no condemnation to me because I am in you (Rom. 8:1).

Every sin, past—present—future, has been forgiven (Eph. 1:7) and cleansed (1 John 1:7) by Your blood.

Your love for me is perfect (1 John 4:18); therefore, I have nothing to fear. Thank you that nothing can touch me unless it is filtered through You, and all things will work for my good and Your glory (Rom. 8:28). Your love for me is unconditional (John 15:9) and everlasting (Jer. 31:3). I open my heart and life to your love; flow that love through me (Rom. 5:5).

You know everything about me (Psalms 139:1-4) and yet You have accepted me just as I am in the beloved (Eph. 1:6).

You made me unique and special to fulfill Your plan (Eph. 2:10).

Thank You for my body, my abilities, my parents which you designed as a part of your perfect plan (Psalms 139:14).

Thank You for the Holy Spirit who lives within me to empower me to obey You (Eph. 3:20).

Thank You that I am complete in You (Col. 2:10).

You have given me all spiritual blessings in Christ (Eph. 1:3).

Your strength is adequate for every task; Your grace is sufficient for every trial (2 Cor. 12:9).

I can do all things through You, Lord Jesus (Phil. 4:13).

Thank You that You will perfect in me Your plan (1 Thess. 5:23-24).

You are faithful even when I am not (2 Tim. 2:13). You have promised never to leave me (Heb. 13:5).

Even now you are changing me bit by bit into your image (2 Cor. 3:18). I will not be foolish by comparing myself with others (2 Cor. 10:12).

Father, how good it is to be Your child. I belong! (1 John 3:1). That makes me Your responsibility (John 15:16).

I give myself completely to You. Whatever is accomplished in and through my life, you'll have to do it (John 15:5; Phil. 2:13).

Thank You for the confidence that You will (Philippians 1:6). Praise, praise be to You!

(Material from Vision Life Ministries)

Prayer to Overcome Performance Orientation

Lord, I have come to see my performance orientation. I confess to You that, although my head believes salvation is by grace, my heart drives me to earn favor, to be good enough to present myself to others and to You.

I admit that I cannot change myself. The fear of not being accepted or loved is so overwhelming it puts me into gear, and I begin performing again.

When acceptance is given with no strings attached, I cannot receive it. I ask You into my heart to do the work in me, for me. Bring my striving to death. I want to rest in Your love. Help me remove the hindrances I have erected which prevent me from entering into Your love.

Lord, I have been angry with You for putting me into this family, this position. I don't want my anger to keep me from You so I ask that You restore my heart. I forgive my family for _____(*List the woundings that helped form performance orientation and those that fueled it*); I ask Your forgiveness for my angry responses, my fear and insecurity, impure motives, and for not believing the truth.
Lord, I renounce the family lies (*name them specifically*):
I accept my identity as Your child. Help me learn how to live that identity in my daily life. Help me to feel, to know within me that "success" is simply being Your child. Help me to be like You, Lord.

I ask You to bring to death in me the structures (the habit patterns of performing) I have created (*be specific*):

_____

I ask You to minister to the ambivalence in me when I want correction but cannot receive it, or when I want and need compliments but cannot believe them. Likewise, be the Lord of my tongue so that wisdom and kindness permeate the corrections and compliments I give. Help me to take my eyes off my needs and fears.

Lord, I resign from managing the universe. I give to You my compulsive need to control people and situations. I recognize I have wounded _____(*list those you know*) by not affirming their contributions – I always had to edit, add, or correct. I could always do it better.

Forgive me, Lord, for both my insecurity and my arrogance, as well as for the wounds I have caused. Help me to believe I am not responsible for all that goes on around me. Forgive me for always being a "Martha," and help me to hear when You call me to be a "Mary." Show me where I have taken on jobs or duties for the wrong reasons, and give me the wisdom to resign from them if necessary.

Help me to fall in love with You, Jesus, so that what others think of me is not important. You have said that it is You working in us that enables us first to will and then to act according to Your good purposes. I want to be a good workman, but only with Your strength and Your will. Help me to be like You, Lord. In Jesus' name, Amen.

(Note: the above prayer was developed by Elijah House and in

Basic I and it is entitled *A prayer to end striving.* Used by permission)

It is important to understand that these sample prayers are not formulas; rather, they offer ideas and guides as the prayer minister is led by the Holy Spirit.

End Notes

i.　　This is a prayer developed by Vision Life Ministries.

ii.　　John Sandford recommends this practice in his Elijah House Basic II School for Prayer Ministry.

iii.　　McClung, Floyd Jr. – The Father Heart of God, Harvest House Publishers, Eugene, OR, 1985

iv.　　Virkler, Mark and Patti, How to Hear God's Voice, Destiny Image Publishers, Inc, Sphippensburg, PA, 2005, and Dialogue with God, Bridge Publishing, Inc. South Plainfield, NJ, 1986

v.　　Virkler, ibid.

vi.　　Vision Life Ministries material

vii.　　Ironside, H. A., Romans and Galatians: An Ironside Expository Commentary, Kregel Publications, 2006

viii.　　Frost, Jack, Spiritual Slavery to Spiritual Sonship, Destiny

Image Publishers, 2006

ix.   Jack Frost, ibid.

x.   A prayer Vision Life Ministries uses to free a person from the orphan spirit

xi.   Robert McCloskey, a quote found on the internet

xii.   Thompson, Carroll, Alienation: Dealing with the Basic Problem of Man, CTM publishing, Dallas, TX, 1994, p. 41

xiii.   John Sanford recommends this practice in his Elijah House Basic I training.

xiv.   Anderson, Neil, Freedom from Fear, Harvest House Publishers, Eugene, OR, 1999, p. 321

xv.   Adapted from an illustration in The Tale of the Tardy Oxcart, by Charles Swindoll, Word Publishing, Nashville, TN, p. 278

xvi.   Malone, Henry

xvii.   Duncan, King, Mule Eggs and Topknots, Seven Worlds Press, Knoxville, TN, 1987, p.291

xviii.   Much of the material in this chapter regarding envy/ jealousy is taken from my book, Conquering Fear, Leland Publications, Allen, TX, 2006.

xix.   Adapted from a Vision Life Ministries prayer

xx.   McClung, Floyd, The Father Heart of God, Harvest House Publishers, Eugene, OR, 1985

xxi. Tournier, Paul, Creative Suffering, SCM-Canterbury Press Limited, 1982

xxii. Oates, Wayne, "On Being a 'Workaholic' (A Serious Jest)". Originally published by World Publishing (New York) in 1971. Reprinted by Abingdon Press (Nashville) in 1972 and 1978. Republished by the Wayne E. Oates Institute in 2004

xxiii. Killinger, Barbara, Workaholics: The Respectable Addicts, New York: Fireside Books, 1992 p. 6

xxiv. Killinger, p.21

xxv. Much of these concepts are taken from Shame: Identity Thief by Dr. Henry Malone

xxvi. From an experience with Vision Life Ministries

xxvii. Pursuit Magazine, Gulf Breeze, FL Vol 3, No 2, 1994. Page 10

xxviii. Pursuit Magazine, Vol 3, No 2. 1994. Page 15

xxix. Virkler, Mark and Patti, Counseled by God, Lamad Publishing, 1989, 2002

xxx. Kylstra, Chester and Betsy, Restoring the Foundations: An Integrated Approach to Healing Ministry, 2nd Edition, Proclaiming His Word Publications, 2001

xxxi. Kylstra, Chester and Betsy

xxxii. Some, but not all, of these concepts are adapted from the writings of Paul Cox, of Alan's Place Ministries.

xxxiii. Paul Cox

xxxiv. Paul Cox

xxxv. Some, but not all, of these concepts are adapted from the writings of Paul Cox, of Alan's Place Ministries.

xxxvi. Paul Cox

xxxvii. Paul Cox

xxxviii. Paul Cox encourages us ministers to, "Ask the Lord that if there is any portion of their being that has been delayed, trapped, captured or imprisoned in another time, another space, dimension or place, as a result of trauma, would He please cause it to be released and rejoined with their core being in this current time, space and dimension. I also ask the Lord to re-unify those portions with the core person. If prompted by the Holy Spirit, walk them through a reunification of these fractured parts by walking them through each dimension or through each year of their lives." Go to www.alansplace.org for an excellent article on healing trauma.

xxxix. Elijah House, Copyright © 1989, 1997, Revised 200, 2001 2002, 2003, 2004, 2009

Don't Forget!

Get the most from this series by purchasing your copy of both the companion book to Soul Pain,

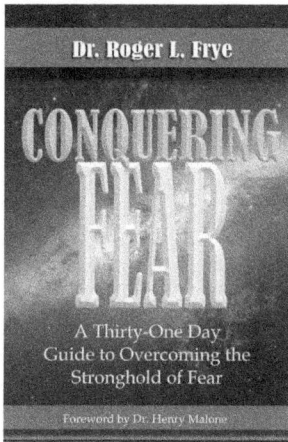

"Conquering Fear"

As well as the

"Leadership Manual"

for this life-changing series!

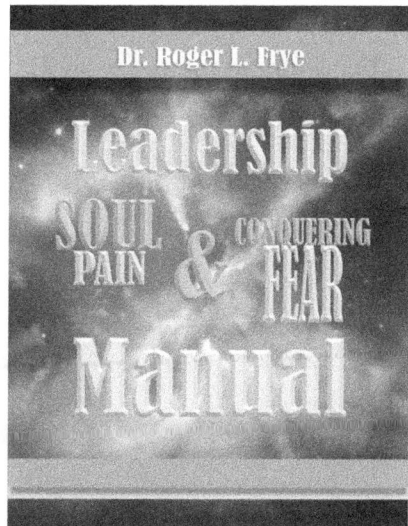

For more information or personal ministry,
contact Roger Frye at 972-984-6043 or
roger.frye@sbcglobal.net